Contents

W9-COS-269

About Daily Geography Practice

Daily Geography Practice is based on the eighteen National Geography Standards and is designed to support any geography and social studies curriculums that you may be using in your classroom.

36 Weekly Sections

Teacher Page

• An answer key for the week is included for easy reference.

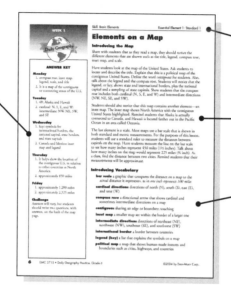

• The national geography element, standard, and skill are included.

• Background information helps the teacher introduce the geography skill.

• Vocabulary words and definitions are given.

Please note that the skills in this book should be taught in direct instruction, and not used as independent practice. Teachers are encouraged to use other reference maps and globes to aid in instruction. Most of the questions can be answered by studying the map or globe. There are some questions, however, that specifically relate to the lesson given by the teacher at the beginning of the week. Review daily the information presented in "Introducing the Map."

Map Page

A map illustrates the geography skills emphasized during the week. Use the map to aid in whole-class instruction, or reproduce a copy for each student to use as a reference for the questions.

Daily Geography Practice • EMC 3715 • © Evan-Moor Corp.

Question Pages

There are two geography questions for each day of the week. The questions progress in difficulty from Monday to Friday. The challenge question at the end of the week asks students to add a feature to the map. Outside references are often required to answer the challenge question.

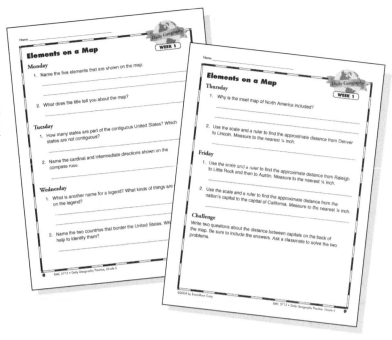

Geography Glossary

Reproduce the glossary pages and cover for students to use as an easy reference booklet throughout the year.

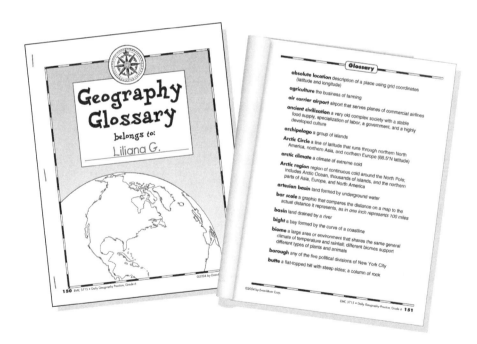

The National Geography Standards

The National Geography Standards includes six essential elements that highlight the major components of geography. Under the six major categories are the eighteen standards that focus on general areas in geography that children are expected to know and understand.

Essential Element 1: The World in Spatial Terms

Geography studies the relationships between people, places, and environments by mapping information about them into a spatial context. The geographically informed person knows and understands the following:

Standard 1 . . . . **Weeks 1–8**
how to use maps and other geographic representations, tools, and technologies to acquire, process, and report information from a spatial perspective,

Standard 2 . . . . **Weeks 9–10**
how to use mental maps to organize information about people, places, and environments in a spatial context, and

Standard 3 . . . . **Weeks 11–12**
how to analyze the spatial organization of people, places, and environments on Earth's surface.

Essential Element 2: Places and Regions

The identities and lives of individuals and peoples are rooted in particular places and in those human constructs called regions. The geographically informed person knows and understands the following:

Standard 4 . . . . **Weeks 13–18**
the physical and human characteristics of places,

Standard 5 . . . . **Weeks 19–22**
that people create regions to interpret Earth's complexity, and

Standard 6 . . . . **Weeks 23–24**
how culture and experience influence people's perceptions of places and regions.

Essential Element 3: Physical Systems

Physical processes shape Earth's surface and interact with plant and animal life to create, sustain, and modify the ecosystems. The geographically informed person knows and understands the following:

Standard 7 . . . . **Week 25**
the physical processes that shape the patterns of Earth's surface, and

Standard 8 . . . . **Week 26**
the characteristics and spatial distribution of ecosystems on Earth's surface.

Essential Element 4: Human Systems

People are central to geography in that human activities help shape Earth's surface, human settlements and structures are part of Earth's surface, and humans compete for control of Earth's surface. The geographically informed person knows and understands the following:

Standard 9 . . . . **Week 27**
the characteristics, distribution, and migration of human populations on Earth's surface,

Standard 10 . . . . **Week 28**
the characteristics, distribution, and complexity of Earth's cultural mosaics,

Standard 11 . . . . **Week 29**
the patterns and networks of economic interdependence on Earth's surface,

Standard 12 . . . . **Week 30**
the processes, patterns, and functions of human settlement, and

Standard 13 . . . . **Week 31**
how the forces of cooperation and conflict among people influence the division and control of Earth's surface.

Essential Element 5: Environment and Society

The physical environment is modified by human activities, largely as a consequence of the ways in which human societies value and use Earth's natural resources. Human activities are also influenced by Earth's physical features and processes. The geographically informed person knows and understands the following:

Standard 14 . . . . **Week 32**
how human actions modify the physical environment,

Standard 15 . . . . **Week 33**
how physical systems affect human systems, and

Standard 16 . . . . **Week 34**
the changes that occur in the meaning, use, distribution, and importance of resources.

Essential Element 6: The Uses of Geography

Knowledge of geography enables people to develop an understanding of the relationships between people, places, and environments over time—that is, of Earth as it was, is, and might be. The geographically informed person knows and understands the following:

Standard 17 . . . . **Week 35**
how to apply geography to interpret the past, and

Standard 18 . . . . **Week 36**
how to apply geography to interpret the present and plan for the future.

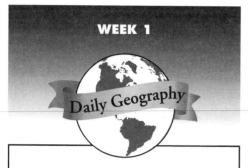

WEEK 1

Daily Geography

Elements on a Map

Introducing the Map

Share with students that as they read a map, they should notice the different elements that are shown such as the title, legend, compass rose, inset map, and scale.

Have students look at the map of the United States. Ask students to locate and describe the title. Explain that this is a political map of the contiguous United States. Define the word *contiguous* for students. Also, talk about the legend and the compass rose. Students will notice that the legend, or key, shows state and international borders, plus the national capital and a sampling of state capitals. Show students that the compass rose includes both cardinal (N, S, E, and W) and intermediate directions (NW, NE, SE, and SW).

Students should also notice that this map contains another element—an inset map. The inset map shows North America with the contiguous United States highlighted. Remind students that Alaska is actually connected to Canada, and Hawaii is located farther out in the Pacific Ocean in an area called Oceania.

The last element is a scale. Most maps use a bar scale that is shown in both standard and metric measurements. For the purposes of this lesson, students will use a standard ruler to measure the distances between capitals on the map. Have students measure the line on the bar scale to see how many inches represent 450 miles (1½ inches). Talk about how many inches on the map would represent 225 miles (¾ inch). As a class, find the distance between two cities. Remind students that their measurements will be approximate.

Introducing Vocabulary

bar scale a graphic that compares the distance on a map to the actual distance it represents, as in *one inch represents 100 miles*

cardinal directions directions of north (N), south (S), east (E), and west (W)

compass rose a directional arrow that shows cardinal and sometimes intermediate directions on a map

contiguous sharing an edge or boundary; touching

inset map a smaller map set within the border of a larger one

intermediate directions directions of northeast (NE), northwest (NW), southeast (SE), and southwest (SW)

international border a border between countries

legend (key) a list that explains the symbols on a map

political map a map that shows human-made features and boundaries such as cities, highways, and countries

Picturing North America

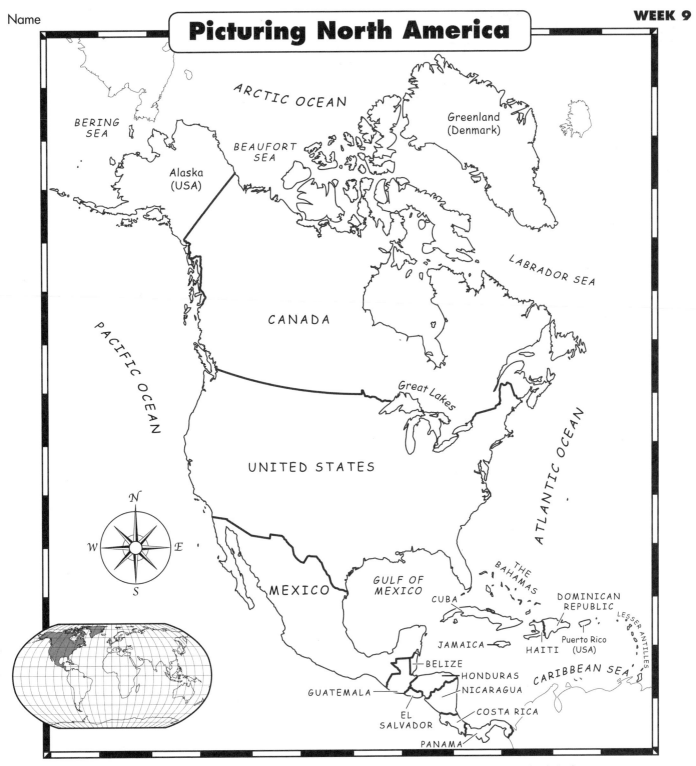

Fifteen of the twenty-three countries are labeled on the map. Puerto Rico, which belongs to the U.S., is also labeled.

The fifteen countries include

- the Bahamas, Canada, Mexico, and the United States;
- the Central American countries of Belize, Costa Rica, El Salvador, Guatemala, Honduras, Nicaragua, and Panama; and
- the Greater Antilles island nations of Cuba, Dominican Republic, Haiti, and Jamaica.

Note: The eight countries and eight dependencies in the Lesser Antilles are not labeled on the map. The eight countries include Antigua and Barbuda, Barbados, Dominica, Grenada, St. Kitts and Nevis, St. Lucia, St. Vincent and the Grenadines, and Trinidad and Tobago.

Daily Geography
WEEK 9

Picturing North America

Monday

1. When you picture a place in your mind, what kind of map are you making?

   _____

2. Don't look at the map of North America. Which country is north of the U.S., and which country is south of the U.S.?

   _____

Tuesday

1. Look at the shape of the United States on the map. Name two states that border the Pacific Ocean.

   _____

2. Look at the shape of the United States. Name two states that border Mexico.

   _____

Wednesday

1. Study the seven countries that make up Central America. Turn over the map and list as many as you can remember.

   _____

   _____

2. Which large island is part of North America, but belongs to a country in Europe? The island territory belongs to which country?

   _____

Picturing North America

Thursday

1. Picture Alaska within the borders of the contiguous United States. Is Alaska smaller, larger, or the same size as Texas?

_____

2. Which island that is labeled in the Greater Antilles is not a country, but rather a part of another country?

_____

Friday

1. Study the Greater Antilles island nations. Turn over the map and name as many as you can remember.

_____

_____

2. Study the waterways that are labeled on the map. Turn over the map and name as many as you can remember.

_____

_____

Challenge

Study the map of North America, making a mental picture of it. Turn the map over. On a blank piece of paper, draw a map sketch of North America. Remember to label as many countries and waterways as you can. Compare your sketch with the map.

WEEK 10

Picturing the World

Introducing the Map

Tell students that there are two different ways to describe where a place is located: by absolute location or by relative location.

Review with students the idea of using grid coordinates to find a place on a map. Tell students that locating places on a map using lines of latitude and longitude is finding the absolute location.

Tell students that when most people look at a map, they use a more informal way of looking at it. They use the skill of relative location. People describe a place using the relation of one place to another. Ask students where the United States is located. They will probably say that the United States is located in North America, between Canada and Mexico. Remind them that what they have just described is the relative location of the United States.

Show students the world map. Talk about the relative location of North America to the rest of the world. This is also a good time to make the connection between the skill of relative location and the ability to make an accurate mental map.

Try looking at other continents in the world, noting their shape, size, and relative location. Talk about the oceans and seas and where they separate the continents. Also, discuss how Asia and Europe are actually one large landmass. Geographers call these two continents Eurasia.

Introducing Vocabulary

absolute location description of a place using grid coordinates (latitude and longitude)

coordinates the latitude and longitude address of a place on a map

Eurasia a landmass made up of the continents of Asia and Europe

mental map a map that a person pictures in his or her mind

relative location description of a place using the relation of one place to another

sea a body of salt water that is part of an ocean, yet is partially enclosed by land

ANSWER KEY

Note: Answers to most questions will not be labeled on the map. Students must use their mental map skills to locate places on the map.

Monday
1. relative location
2. Africa, Antarctica, Asia, Australia, Europe, North America, and South America; Atlantic, Arctic, Indian, Pacific, and Southern Oceans

Tuesday
1. Atlantic, east of North America; Arctic, north of North America; and Pacific Ocean, west of North America
2. Beaufort, Bering, and Labrador Seas

Wednesday
1. The two continents are actually one large landmass.
2. Australia; Tasman Sea

Thursday
1. Philippine Sea, Sea of Japan, Sea of Okhotsk, and South China Sea
2. Italy/Europe; India/Asia; and Japan/Asia

Friday
1. Black and Caspian Seas; Barents, Mediterranean, and North Seas
2. Beaufort and Labrador Seas, and the Atlantic, Arctic, and Pacific Oceans

Challenge
The map sketch of the world should resemble the shapes of the continents, and the locations of the continents should be in the correct relative direction. Students should label at least the seven continents and five oceans, plus a few seas.

Name

Picturing the World

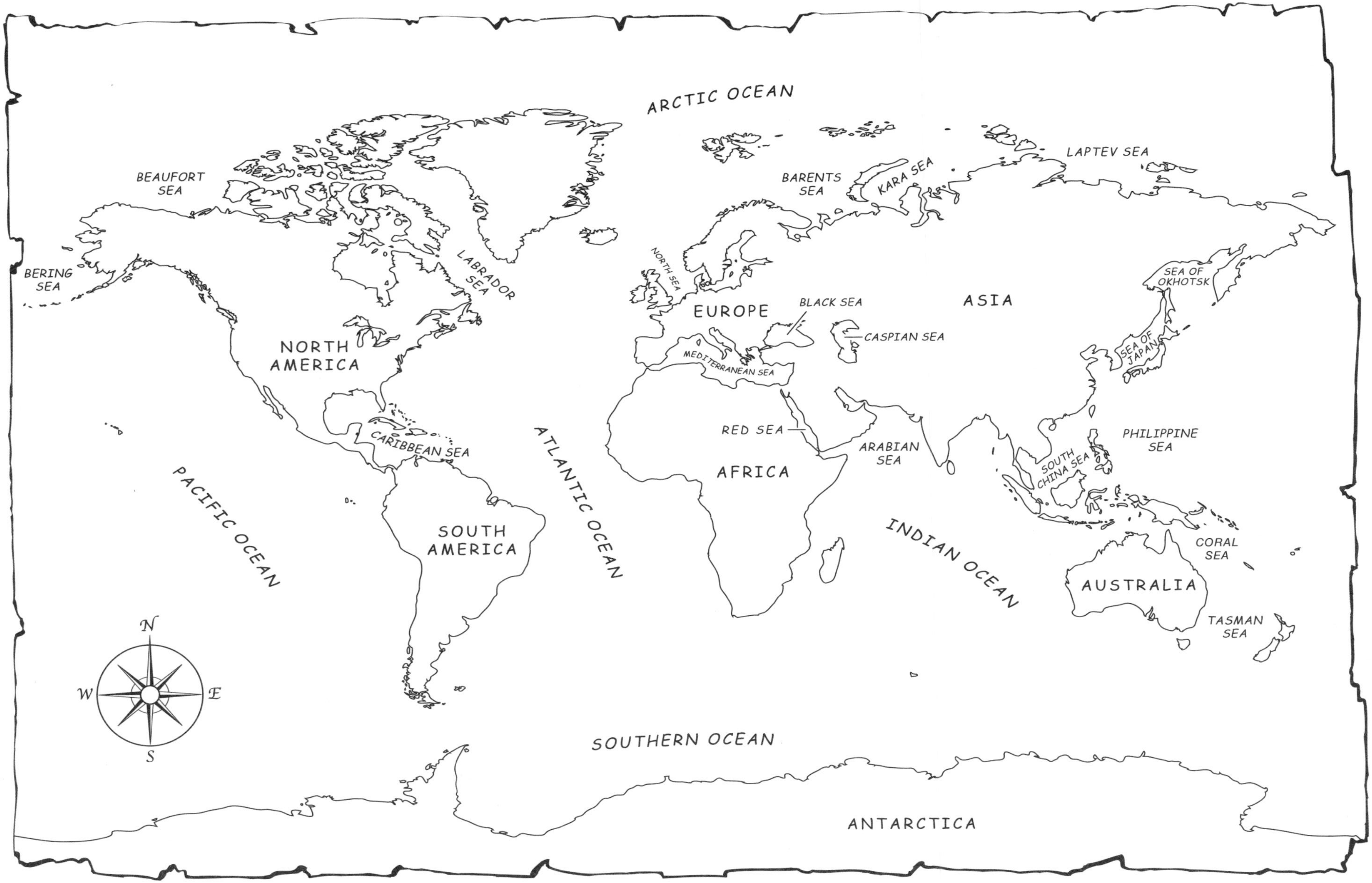

ARCTIC OCEAN

BEAUFORT SEA

NORTH AMERICA

BERING SEA

LABRADOR SEA

CARIBBEAN SEA

SOUTH AMERICA

PACIFIC OCEAN

ATLANTIC OCEAN

LAPTEV SEA

BARENTS SEA

KARA SEA

ASIA

EUROPE

NORTH SEA

MEDITERRANEAN SEA

BLACK SEA

CASPIAN SEA

RED SEA

ARABIAN SEA

AFRICA

INDIAN OCEAN

SEA OF OKHOTSK

SEA OF JAPAN

PHILIPPINE SEA

SOUTH CHINA SEA

CORAL SEA

TASMAN SEA

AUSTRALIA

SOUTHERN OCEAN

ANTARCTICA

N E W S

Picturing the World

Monday

1. Look at the world map. Is it possible to find the absolute location or the relative location of the seven continents?

_____

2. Look at the world map. Turn it over and name the seven continents and five oceans of the world.

_____

_____

Tuesday

1. Which oceans border North America, and in which directions are they in relation to the continent?

_____

_____

2. Which labeled seas border North America?

_____

_____

Wednesday

1. Why are the continents of Europe and Asia sometimes referred to as Eurasia?

_____

2. Which continent is called both a continent and a country? Which sea separates this area from New Zealand?

_____

Picturing the World

Thursday

1. Name all the labeled seas that lie on the east coast of Asia.

    _____

    _____

2. The countries of Italy, India, and Japan are easy to picture due to their unique shapes. In which continents are they located?

    _____

    _____

Friday

1. Name two inland seas that are located in Europe. Name two seas in Europe that flow into an ocean.

    _____

    _____

2. Name the labeled waterways that border Canada.

    _____

    _____

    _____

Challenge

Think about the relative locations and sizes of the continents, oceans, and seas. Turn over the map. On a blank piece of paper, draw the world map from memory. Label as many continents, oceans, and seas as you can remember. Compare your map sketch with the world map.

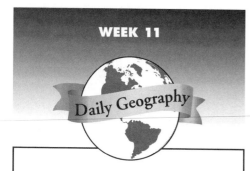

A Road Map: Wyoming

Introducing the Map

Show students the road map of Wyoming. Talk about the primary roads. Define *primary roads* as major interstate highways and U.S. highways. Tell students that these highways have special symbols and numbers. Look at the legend to see the symbol for an interstate highway. Have students name the interstate highways of Wyoming. Tell them that each interstate highway is part of a national network of connected roads. Interstate routes that go east and west have even numbers. North-south interstate routes have odd numbers. Students will also notice squares where interstate highways meet other highways. These are called highway interchanges. Look at the symbol for a highway interchange.

Then have students notice the U.S. highways shown on the map. Again look at the legend to see the symbol. Tell students that this map shows a sampling of U.S. highways in the state. U.S. highways are also a part of a national network of connected roads. Also, share with students that when two highways merge into one, both numbers are shown.

Students should also notice that there is a scale on the map. Tell students that a scale compares the distance on a map to the actual distance it represents. Most maps use a bar scale, which is shown in both standard and metric measurements. For the purposes of this lesson, students will use standard measurements.

The map of Wyoming uses a scale of 2 inches to represent 100 miles. As a class, find the distance between two cities. The strategy of using string to measure the distance is helpful because the roads are not straight lines. Then the students can measure the string with a ruler and use the scale to figure out the distance in miles. Remind students that their measurements will be estimates.

Tell students that there are numerous state and county roads in Wyoming, which are called secondary roads, but that they are not represented on this map. In fact, Wyoming has more than 37,000 miles of roads and highways through this large state.

ANSWER KEY

Monday
1. interstate and U.S. highways
2. Interstates 25, 80, and 90; Interstate 80

Tuesday
1. Cheyenne, Wheatland, Casper, Douglas, Buffalo, and Sheridan
2. Buffalo; highway interchange

Wednesday
1. west on U.S. Highway 20/26 to Riverton, continue on U.S. Highway 26 west and merge onto U.S. Highway 26/287 to Grand Teton National Park
2. west on Interstate 90 to Buffalo and then north on Interstate 90; or north on U.S. Highway 14/16 and northwest on U.S. Highway 14

Thursday
1. Traveling south on Interstate 25 and then west on Interstate 80 would probably be the fastest route.
2. Interstates 25 and 80 and U.S Highway 85

Friday
1. 14, 16, 20, 89, 191, and 287; Students may say 26, but that highway actually breaks away to Grand Teton National Park.
2. about 350 to 375 miles

Challenge
Answers will vary. One possible question might be: What is the mileage between Rawlins and Rock Springs? (Answer: about 100 miles)

Introducing Vocabulary

bar scale a graphic that compares the distance on a map to the actual distance it represents, as in *one inch represents 100 miles*

highway interchange a place where major roads meet or join

interstate highway a major public road that is part of a nationwide highway system; the interstate highway system was created after the U.S. highway system

mileage total number of miles traveled

road map a map for motorists that shows the highways of an area

U.S. highway a major public road that is part of a nationwide highway system; the U.S. highway system was created before the interstate highway system

Name

A Road Map

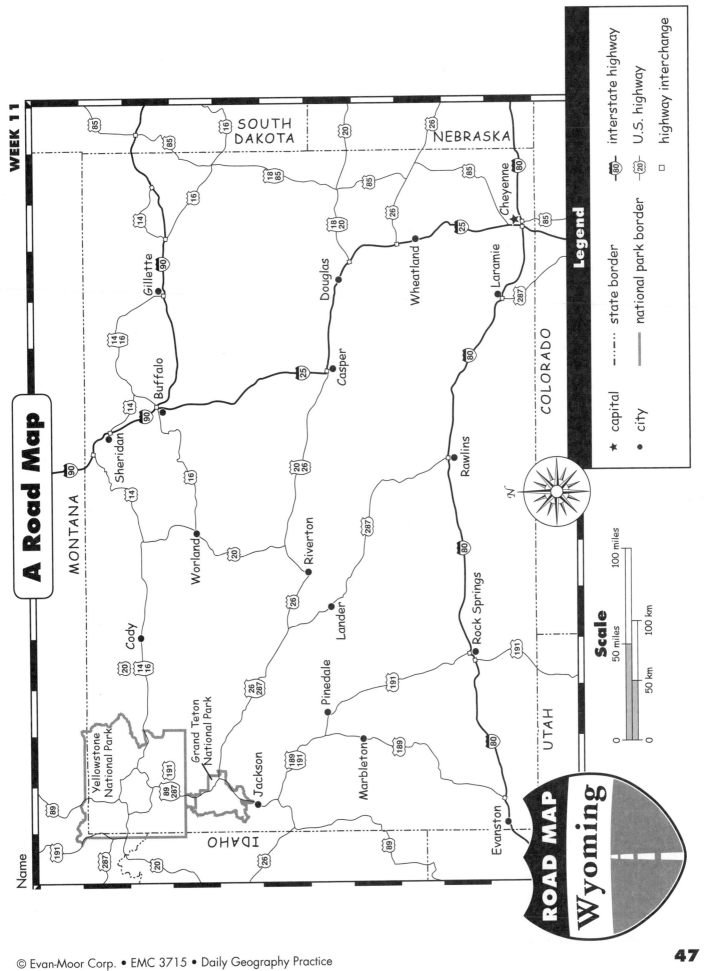

Legend

- ★ capital
- • city
- □ highway interchange
- ····· state border
- —— national park border
- 🛡️80 interstate highway
- ◯20 U.S. highway

Scale

50 miles   100 miles

50 km   100 km

ROAD MAP
Wyoming

A Road Map: Wyoming

Monday

1. There are two major kinds of roads on the map. What are they called?

   _____

2. Name the three interstate highways. Which interstate highway travels in an east-west direction across the state?

   _____

Tuesday

1. Name the cities that are along the north-south portions of Interstates 25 and 90.

   _____

   _____

2. At which city do Interstate 25 and Interstate 90 intersect? What is the marking called at this intersection?

   _____

Wednesday

1. Which direct route would a person travel from Casper to the Grand Teton National Park?

   _____

   _____

2. Which two routes could a person take from Gillette to Sheridan?

   _____

   _____

A Road Map: Wyoming

Thursday

1. Interstate highways usually have higher speed limits than U.S. highways. Which is the fastest route from Casper to Rawlins?

   _____

2. Which highways' interchange is at Wyoming's capital?

   _____

Friday

1. Which highways connect with Yellowstone National Park?

   _____

2. Using the scale, estimate the distance in miles of Interstate 80 within the borders of Wyoming.

   _____

Challenge

Make up two math problems using the map and map scale of Wyoming. Write your questions and answers on the back of the map. Ask a classmate to solve your problems.

WEEK 12

ANSWER KEY

Monday

1. At least five of the following: airplane, automobile, bus, train, pedestrian walkway, taxi, truck, or van
2. 3 terminals and 8 concourses; international terminal

Tuesday

1. Lower Road
2. pedestrian tunnel

Wednesday

1. a train system called the Chicago Transit Authority (CTA) or the Airport Transit System (ATS)
2. Parking Lot A

Thursday

1. Airport Transit System
2. 57,600 passengers

Friday

1. 56,615,214 passengers
2. Two-step problem:
   60 ÷ 7= 8.57;
   8.57 ÷ 2 trips = 4.28, or
   4 round trips an hour

Challenge

Answers will vary. Two possible questions might be: Find the average number of passengers that have been served by O'Hare from 2001 to 2010. Has O'Hare seen an overall increase or decrease in the number of passengers over the last five years?

Skill: Routes — Essential Element 1: Standard 3

Chicago O'Hare International Airport

Introducing the Map

Ask students if they have ever flown on an airplane. Discuss the fact that air travel has become the chief means of long-distance transportation. Every day, the world's airports handle millions of passengers and thousands of commercial airplanes for both business and tourist travel.

The largest airports look like small cities. Airplanes approach and take off on assigned routes called traffic patterns. Air traffic controllers use radar, radio, and signal lights to direct the air traffic. Cars, buses, and taxis pick up or drop off passengers. Major airports have rapid transit, which are trains that carry passengers to and from designated areas. Passengers rush to the right terminal and then to the gate to board airplanes. Thousands of people such as the pilots, ticket agents, baggage carriers, and airport security personnel work at the airport. People also work in places like restaurants, shops, and other services.

Tell students these facts about O'Hare as they look at the diagram of the airport:

- Chicago O'Hare International Airport's call letters are ORD (Ordway). Those initials appear on airline tickets and are used when booking flights.
- O'Hare served 66,565,952 passengers in 2002. O'Hare consistently ranks as the second-busiest airport in the world. Atlanta's Hartsfield Airport ranks first.
- Forty-six commercial airlines serve O'Hare, both domestically and internationally. A few airlines are American, British Airways, Continental, Delta, Northwest, Singapore, and United Airlines.
- O'Hare has four main terminals with concourses at each terminal.
- The Airport Transit System (ATS) is a train system that connects all terminals. It is a free 24-hour service, which can carry up to 2,400 passengers per hour from Terminal 1 to Lot E. The train trip from Terminal 1 to Lot E takes just seven minutes. The Chicago Transit Authority (CTA) runs a 24-hour train service from the airport to Chicago, running every ten minutes. Free shuttle buses are also available to transport passengers.
- The airport is located on Interstate 190, about 40 minutes from central Chicago.

Introducing Vocabulary

air carrier airport airport that serves planes of commercial airlines

cargo all freight, except baggage, carried by an airplane

concourse a large open space for passage of crowds

control tower a glass-enclosed booth equipped with radar, radio, signal lights, and other equipment for directing air traffic

gate an airport terminal entryway used for boarding or leaving an airplane

terminal a main airport building for passenger services

traffic pattern a pattern of flight around an airport for arriving and departing aircraft

Name

Chicago O'Hare International Airport

Chicago O'Hare International Airport (ORD) is the second-busiest airport in the world. Over 66,500,000 passengers travel through the airport each year.

N

Parking Lot F (closed)

P

Parking Lot E

P

Rental Car Lots

Airport Transit System (ATS)

12 45

Parking Lot G

P

Parking Lot D

P

190

Chicago Transit Authority (CTA)

International Terminal 5

Parking Lot C

P

Lower Road (Arrivals)

Upper Road (Departures)

Pedestrian Passages

Parking Lot B

P

Parking Lot A

P

•Concourse L

•Concourse K

•Terminal 3

•Concourse H

•Concourse G

•Concourse B

•Concourse C

Pedestrian Tunnel

▲Concourse F

•Terminal 1

▲Concourse E

▲Terminal 2

Chicago O'Hare International Airport

Monday

1. Name at least five different modes of transportation at Chicago O'Hare International Airport.

   _____

   _____

2. How many terminals and concourses are located in the main connected part of the airport? Which terminal stands alone?

   _____

   _____

Tuesday

1. If a person were picking up a passenger at Terminal 3, would he or she take the Lower Road or the Upper Road?

   _____

2. How does a person get from Concourse B to Concourse C in Terminal 1?

   _____

Wednesday

1. A person can drive on Interstate 190 to the airport. What other means of travel parallels the interstate highway?

   _____

2. If a person were traveling out of Concourse L in Terminal 3 and through the pedestrian passages, which parking lot would he or she be closest to?

Chicago O'Hare International Airport

Thursday

1. If a person wanted to rent a car at the airport, which means of travel would take him or her to the rental car lots?

   _____

2. If the ATS train system can carry 2,400 passengers per hour, how many passengers could it carry in a 24-hour period?

   _____

Friday

1. In 2010, O'Hare served 67,026,191 domestic and international passengers. If there were 10,410,977 international passengers, how many domestic passengers were there?

   _____

2. It only takes seven minutes for an ATS train to travel from Terminal 1 to Lot E. How many round trips can the train make in one hour?

   _____

Challenge

The following statistics show the number of passengers that have been served by O'Hare from 2006 through 2010.

Year	Total Number of Passengers
2006	76,282,212
2007	76,182,025
2008	70,819,015
2009	64,397,782
2010	67,026,191

Using these statistics, write two math problems on the back of the map. Be sure to include the answers. Then have a classmate solve the problems.

WEEK 13

Daily Geography

ANSWER KEY

Monday

1. Any four of the following: deserts, islands, mountains, peninsulas, plains, and shield

2. Any four of the following: bays, gulfs, lakes, oceans, rivers or seas

Tuesday

1. Rocky Mountains; Canada, United States, and Mexico (Sierra Madres are an extension of the Rockies.)

2. Atlantic, Arctic, and Pacific Oceans; Beaufort, Bering, Labrador, and Caribbean Seas; Labrador and Caribbean Seas

Wednesday

1. Missouri River and Mississippi River

2. Interior Plains and Great Plains

Thursday

1. Greater and Lesser Antilles

2. Gulf of Alaska, Gulf of California, Gulf of Mexico, and Gulf of St. Lawrence; Gulf of Mexico and Gulf of St. Lawrence

Friday

1. peninsula; Mexico

2. Canadian Shield

Challenge

Lake Erie, Lake Huron, Lake Michigan, Lake Ontario, and Lake Superior

Mt. McKinley 20,320 feet (6,194 m); Death Valley 282 feet (86 m) below sea level

A Physical Map: North America

Introducing the Map

Discuss with students that physical maps show the natural landforms and waterways on Earth's surface. Share the following information with students as they look at the physical map of North America.

North America has the following main land regions:

- The Coast Ranges extend from Alaska to Mexico. Familiar mountain ranges in this area are the Alaska Range, Olympic Mountains, the Cascade Range, and the Sierra Nevada Range.

- Deserts lie between the mountain ranges. They are the Great Basin, Mojave, and the Sonoran Deserts. The Chihuahuan Desert extends from southern New Mexico and Texas into Mexico.

- The Rocky Mountains run from Alaska to New Mexico, and extend southward into Mexico. In Mexico, they are called the Sierra Madres.

- The Interior Plains cover much of central Canada and the North-Central region of the United States. The driest western part is called the Great Plains.

- The Canadian Shield is a large area of ancient rock that covers most of eastern Canada.

- The Appalachian Mountains extend from Quebec to Alabama. Some familiar mountains in this range are the White Mountains, Green Mountains, and the Catskill Mountains.

- Coastal lowlands stretch along the Atlantic Ocean and the Gulf of Mexico.

- Central America is an isthmus that connects the southern part of North America to South America.

- Most of the islands in the Caribbean Sea were formed by volcanoes.

Also, discuss the major waterways that are labeled on the map. Due to the wide variety of physical features in North America, only major ones were included.

Introducing Vocabulary

Canadian Shield a U-shaped region of ancient rock that curves around the Hudson Bay; southern part of shield is thick with forests and northern part is tundra

desert a dry region with little or no rainfall

Greater Antilles an island group of the West Indies including Cuba, Jamaica, Hispaniola (Dominican Republic and Haiti), and Puerto Rico (U.S.)

gulf a large area of ocean that is partly surrounded by land

isthmus a narrow strip of land having water on each side and connecting two larger bodies of land

Lesser Antilles an island group of the West Indies including eight countries and eight dependencies

mountain range a group or chain of mountains

physical map a map that shows natural landforms and waterways on Earth's surface

plains a large flat area of land

A Physical Map: North America

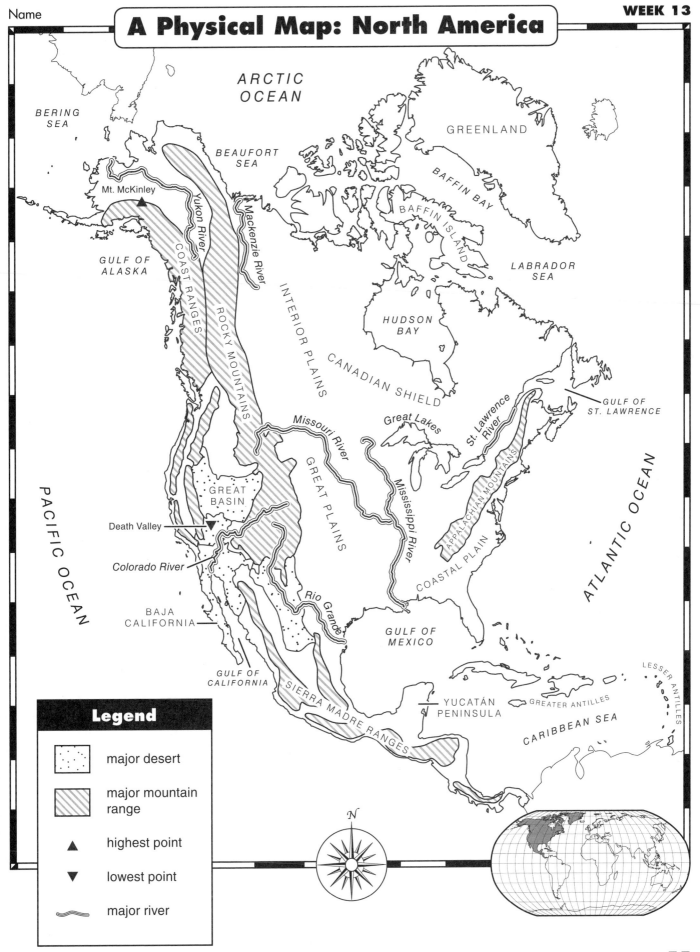

Legend

major desert

major mountain range

▲ highest point

▼ lowest point

major river

A Physical Map: North America

Monday

1. Name four kinds of landforms that are shown on the map.

   _____

2. Name four kinds of waterways that are shown on the map.

   _____

Tuesday

1. Which mountain range is the largest in North America? It extends through which three countries in North America?

   _____

   _____

2. Name the labeled oceans and seas that border North America. Which seas flow into the Atlantic Ocean?

   _____

   _____

Wednesday

1. Which two rivers in the U.S. make up the longest river system in North America?

   _____

2. Which labeled landforms cover most of central Canada and the central United States?

   _____

   _____

A Physical Map: North America

Thursday

1. Which two groups of islands are located in the Caribbean Sea?

   _____

2. Name the labeled gulfs. Which one is the largest, and which one is connected by water to one of the Great Lakes?

   _____

   _____

   _____

Friday

1. What kind of landform is Baja California? Is it located in Mexico or the United States?

   _____

2. Which U-shaped region of ancient rock curves around the Hudson Bay?

   _____

Challenge

On the map page, label the names of the five Great Lakes. Also, write the elevations for Mt. McKinley, the highest point, and Death Valley, the lowest point, on the map. Use a reference physical map to find the elevations.

ANSWER KEY

Monday
1. Andes Mountains
2. 6; Orinoco River

Tuesday
1. Mount Aconcagua; 22,831 feet (6,959 m)
2. Valdéz Peninsula; ⁻131 ft./⁻40 m

Wednesday
1. Patagonia; Pampas grasslands and Andes Mountains
2. Amazon River; Madeira and Tapajós Rivers

Thursday
1. Strait of Magellan and the Drake Passage
2. Galápagos Islands, northwest; Marajó Island, northeast; Falkland Islands, southeast; Tierra del Fuego, southeast

Friday
1. through the Strait of Magellan into the Pacific Ocean; or around Cape Horn into the Drake Passage and then into the Pacific Ocean
2. south in the Atlantic through the Drake Passage and into Pacific Ocean; north into the Caribbean Sea, through the Panama Canal, and into Pacific Ocean

Challenge
Students should color much of northern South America, including the areas around the Amazon Basin, and around the Amazon, Madeira, and Tapajós Rivers.

A Physical Map: South America

Introducing the Map

Review with students the definition of a physical map. Have students name a few typical landforms and waterways that are shown on a physical map.

Show students the physical map of South America. Discuss the different landforms and waterways shown on the map. Remind students that only major physical features are shown. Students may be unfamiliar with the terms *basin*, *cape*, and *strait,* so define these terms for them. There are also Spanish terms for the different land areas that make up the large region called the Central Plains. The *Llanos* and the *Pampas* are areas that are made up of rolling grasslands. The *Gran Chaco* area is made up of scrub forests. The *Tierra del Fuego* is a group of islands at the tip of South America. Be sure to also define the word *Patagonia* for students. Patagonia is a dry, grassy region.

As students look at the physical map of South America, share these interesting facts about the continent:

- Angel Falls in Venezuela has a longer drop than any other waterfall in the world.
- The Amazon River is the second-longest river in the world.
- The Andes Mountains are the world's longest mountain range.
- The Atacama Desert is one of the driest places in the world.
- The Galápagos Islands belong to Ecuador. They are home to huge sea turtles and other unusual animals.
- The world's largest rainforest is located in the Amazon River Basin.

Also, have students look at the inset map of the world to understand the relative location of South America.

Introducing Vocabulary

archipelago a group of islands

basin land drained by a river

cape a point of land that extends into a sea or an ocean

elevation height of the land above sea level

mountain range a group or chain of mountains

passage another name for a channel, or a body of water joining two larger bodies of water

physical map a map that shows natural landforms and waterways on Earth's surface

strait a narrow channel connecting two bodies of water

tributary a small stream or river that flows into a larger one

A Physical Map: South America

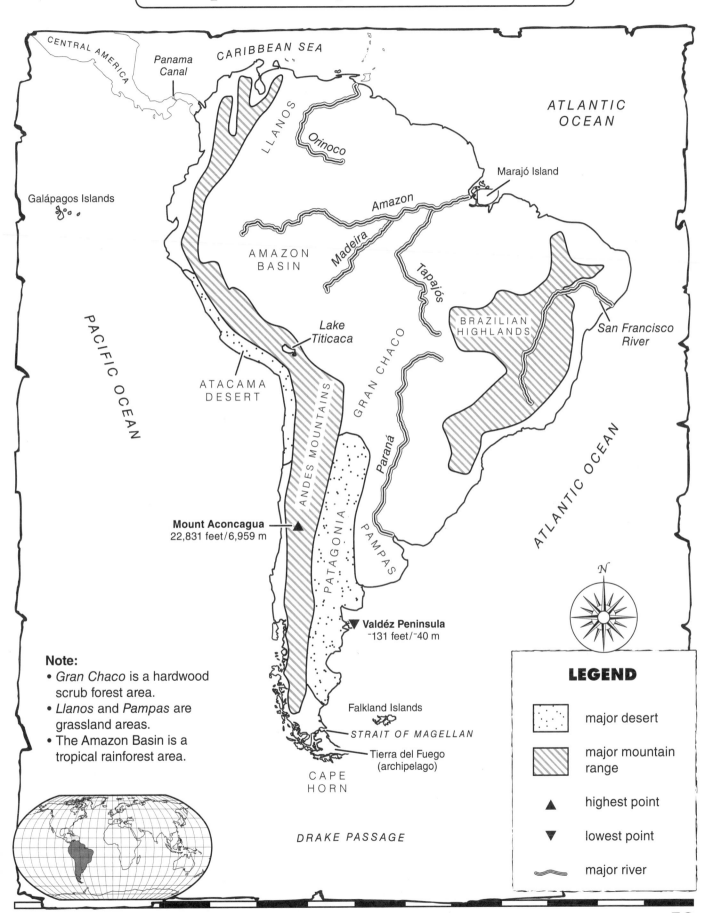

PACIFIC OCEAN

CENTRAL AMERICA

Panama Canal

CARIBBEAN SEA

ATLANTIC OCEAN

LLANOS

Orinoco

Galápagos Islands

Amazon

Marajó Island

AMAZON BASIN

Madeira

Tapajós

BRAZILIAN HIGHLANDS

San Francisco River

Lake Titicaca

GRAN CHACO

ATACAMA DESERT

ANDES MOUNTAINS

Paraná

ATLANTIC OCEAN

Mount Aconcagua
22,831 feet / 6,959 m

PATAGONIA

PAMPAS

▼ **Valdéz Peninsula**
-131 feet / -40 m

N

Note:
- *Gran Chaco* is a hardwood scrub forest area.
- *Llanos* and *Pampas* are grassland areas.
- The Amazon Basin is a tropical rainforest area.

Falkland Islands

STRAIT OF MAGELLAN

Tierra del Fuego (archipelago)

CAPE HORN

DRAKE PASSAGE

LEGEND

major desert

major mountain range

▲ highest point

▼ lowest point

major river

Daily Geography
WEEK 14

A Physical Map: South America

Monday

1. Name the longest mountain range in South America and in the world.

   _____

2. How many rivers are labeled on the map? Which river flows into the Caribbean Sea?

   _____

Tuesday

1. What is the name of the highest mountain in South America? What is its elevation?

   _____

2. Where is the lowest elevation found? What is its elevation?

   _____

Wednesday

1. Which desert covers more land area in South America? The desert is located between which two landforms?

   _____

2. Which river is the longest in South America? Which two rivers are tributaries of this river?

   _____

Daily Geography Practice • EMC 3715 • © Evan-Moor Corp.

A Physical Map: South America

Thursday

1. The Tierra del Fuego is an archipelago, or group of islands. They are located between which two labeled waterways?

   _____

2. Name the islands that are labeled on the map. Give their locations in relation to Mount Aconcagua.

   _____

   _____

   _____

Friday

1. If a person sailed from the Falkland Islands to the Galápagos Islands, in which two ways could he or she travel?

   _____

   _____

2. If a person sailed from Marajó Island to the Galápagos Islands, in which two ways could he or she travel?

   _____

   _____

Challenge

The Amazon Rainforest covers almost two million square miles (5.2 mil. sq. km) in the Amazon River Basin. About two-thirds of the rainforest lies in Brazil. The rainforest also lies in parts of Bolivia, Peru, Ecuador, Colombia, and Venezuela.

Color the Amazon Rainforest area on the map of South America. Use a reference physical map or other resource to help you.

WEEK 15

Daily Geography

A Physical Map: Australia

Introducing the Map

Share with students the definition of a physical map. Have students name a few typical landforms and waterways that are shown on a physical map.

Show students the physical map of Australia. Discuss the different landforms and waterways shown on the map. Remind students that only major physical features are given. Share the following information about Australia as they study the map:

- Australia is the only country that is also called a continent. It is sometimes referred to as the "island continent." Australia is the sixth-largest country in the world and the smallest continent in terms of size.

- Australia is located between the Pacific Ocean and the Indian Ocean. Cartographers refer to the southern part of the Indian Ocean as the Southern Ocean.

- Most of Australia is low and flat. However, the Great Dividing Range includes some of the highest elevations in Australia. The Australian Alps at the end of the range include the highest peak of Mount Kosciuszko.

- The country has four major deserts—the Gibson, Great Sandy, Great Victoria, and the Simpson Deserts.

- Another interesting feature is the Great Artesian Basin. This underground water area has allowed a major part of arid Australia to be settled and turned into grazing lands.

- The Great Barrier Reef is a chain of more than 2,500 reefs. It is 1,250 miles (2,012 km) long. It also includes many small islands. The reefs have about 400 species of corals of many colors and sizes.

- The Great Australian Bight is a wide bay which indents South Australia. The bay is 720 miles (1,159 km) long.

Introducing Vocabulary

artesian basin land formed by underground water

bight a bay formed by the curve of a coastline

cartographer mapmaker

coral a substance made up of skeletons of tiny sea creatures

coral reef a ridge made of coral and other materials that have solidified into rock

elevation height of the land above sea level

gulf a large area of ocean that is partly surrounded by land

mountain range a group or chain of mountains

physical map a map that shows natural landforms and waterways on Earth's surface

strait a narrow channel connecting two bodies of water

tableland a high, broad, level plateau

ANSWER KEY

Monday
1. Indian, Pacific, and Southern Oceans; Coral, Tasman, and Timor Seas
2. Gibson, Great Sandy, Great Victoria, and Simpson Deserts

Tuesday
1. Australian Alps
2. Melville Island and Tasmania

Wednesday
1. Murray River; southeast Australia
2. Lake Eyre, Lake Mackay, Darling River, Murray River, and Victoria River; Some students may say Great Artesian Basin, which is an underground water area.

Thursday
1. Bass Strait
2. The Great Barrier Reef; off the northeast coast of Australia.

Friday
1. Gulf of Carpentaria and the Great Australian Bight
2. Barkly Tableland

Challenge
Lake Eyre is 52 ft. (16 m) below sea level; Mount Kosciuszko is 7,310 ft. (2,228 m) above sea level.

Name

A Physical Map: Australia

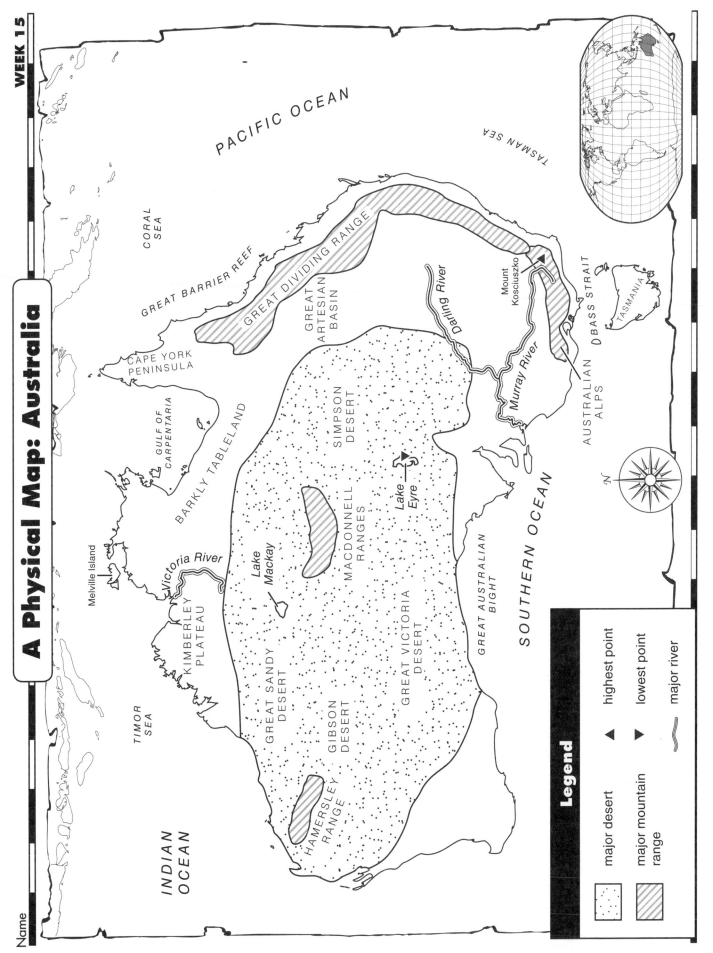

PACIFIC OCEAN

CORAL SEA

GREAT BARRIER REEF

GREAT DIVIDING RANGE

GREAT ARTESIAN BASIN

Darling River

Mount Kosciuszko

AUSTRALIAN ALPS

TASMAN SEA

BASS STRAIT

TASMANIA

Murray River

CAPE YORK PENINSULA

GULF OF CARPENTARIA

BARKLY TABLELAND

SIMPSON DESERT

MACDONNELL RANGES

Lake Eyre

SOUTHERN OCEAN

GREAT AUSTRALIAN BIGHT

GREAT VICTORIA DESERT

Victoria River

Melville Island

KIMBERLEY PLATEAU

Lake Mackay

GREAT SANDY DESERT

GIBSON DESERT

HAMERSLEY RANGE

TIMOR SEA

INDIAN OCEAN

Legend

▲ highest point

▶ lowest point

〰 major river

▫ major desert

▨ major mountain range

Daily Geography

WEEK 15

A Physical Map: Australia

Monday

1. Australia is a large island continent. Which labeled oceans and seas surround the continent?

   _____

   _____

2. Australia has four major deserts. Name them.

   _____

   _____

Tuesday

1. Which mountains are on the south end of the Great Dividing Range?

   _____

2. Which labeled islands are part of the continent of Australia?

   _____

Wednesday

1. Which river is the longest in Australia? Where is it located?

   _____

2. Name five inland waterways of Australia.

   _____

   _____

A Physical Map: Australia

Thursday

1. What is the area on the map called that is a strip of water that connects the Tasman Sea with the Southern Ocean?

_____

2. What is the name of the long chain of coral reefs, and where is it located in Australia?

_____

_____

Friday

1. Name the two large areas of the ocean that are partly surrounded by land.

_____

_____

2. Which landform is a high, broad, level plateau—the Barkly Tableland or the Great Artesian Basin?

_____

Challenge

The lowest and highest points of Australia are labeled on the map. Find out the elevations of Lake Eyre and Mount Kosciuszko and write them on the map. Use a reference physical map to help you.

ANSWER KEY

Monday

1. 8; Appalachian Mountains, Rocky Mountains, and the Andes Mountains

2. Alps, Atlas, Caucasus, Himalaya, and Ural Mountains

Tuesday

1. Atlas Mountains; Kilimanjaro is an isolated peak in east Africa (Tanzania).

2. Mount Everest, Himalaya

Wednesday

1. Ural Mountains

2. Mount Elbrus

Thursday

1. Three of the following: Alaska, Aleutian, Cascade, Coast, and Sierra Nevada Ranges

2. Kilimanjaro, Mount Kosciuszko, and Vinson Massif

Friday

1. They are all volcanic mountains that have erupted.

2. Mid-Atlantic Ridge, located below sea level

Challenge

Mountain	Location	Height in Feet and Meters
1. Mt. Everest	Nepal/Tibet border	29,035 ft./8,850 m
2. Aconcagua	Argentina	22,831 ft./6,959 m
3. Mt. McKinley	Alaska	20,320 ft./6,194 m
4. Kilimanjaro	Tanzania	19,331 ft./5,892 m
5. Mount Elbrus	Russia	18,510 ft./5,642 m
6. Vinson Massif	Antarctica	16,864 ft./5,140 m
7. Mt. Kosciuszko	Australia	7,310 ft./2,228 m

Mountain Ranges of the World

Introducing the Map

Explain to students that there are physical maps that show specific landforms such as the major mountain ranges. Define a mountain, a mountain range, and a mountain system. Further explain that a mountain may be a single peak, or it may be part of a mountain range. A group of mountain ranges form a larger mountain system. Explain to students that the largest mountain system in the world is actually undersea. It is called the Mid-Atlantic Ridge. It stretches more than 10,000 miles (16,000 km) from the Northern Atlantic Ocean to Antarctica.

When people talk about major mountain systems, however, they usually are referring to ones above sea level. The height of most mountains is given as the distance that its peak rises above sea level. For example, the world's highest mountain is Mount Everest at 29,035 feet (8,850 m) above sea level.

As students look at the map of the mountain ranges, share the following information with them:

There are five major mountain systems in the world. North America has three of the major systems—the Appalachian Mountains, the Pacific Mountain System, and the Rocky Mountains. The Appalachian Mountains stretch from the Gaspe Peninsula in Canada to Alabama. The Pacific Mountain System stretches along the west coast of North America. It includes the Coast Ranges, the Sierra Nevada of California, the Cascade Range of Oregon, and the Alaska and Aleutian Ranges in Alaska. The Rocky Mountains extend through Mexico, the United States, and Canada.

In South America, the Andes Mountains is the longest mountain system in the world. It stretches along the west coast of the continent.

The Tethyan Mountain System extends across Africa, Europe, and Asia. It includes the Atlas Mountains of Africa, the Alps and Carpathian Mountains in Europe, and the Caucasus Mountains on the border of Europe and Asia. The Tethyan Mountain System also includes the Zagros Mountains, the Pamirs, the Karakoram Range, and the Himalaya in Asia.

Tell students that only a sampling of the major mountain ranges are included on the map, and the highest mountain for each continent is shown on the map.

Introducing Vocabulary

mountain any point of land that rises quickly to at least 1,000 feet above its surroundings

mountain peak the summit, or highest point, of a mountain

mountain range a group or chain of mountains

mountain system a group of mountain ranges

physical map a map that shows natural landforms and waterways on Earth's surface

Mountain Ranges of the World

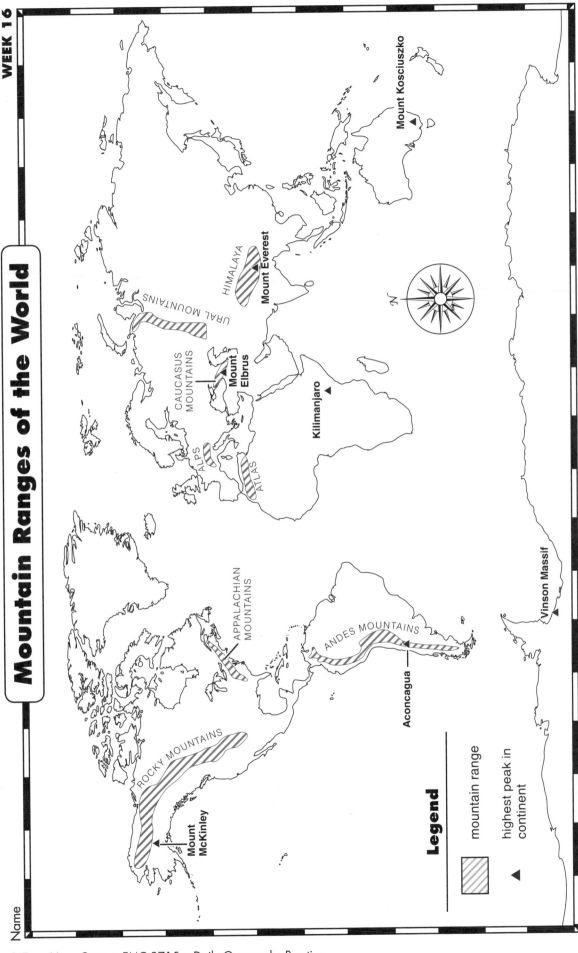

North America has three major mountain systems. The Appalachian Mountains and the Rocky Mountains are well known. North America also has the Pacific Mountain System. This system consists of two parallel chains of mountains that run from southern California to Alaska. Names of the mountain ranges include the Alaska and Aleutian Ranges, the Cascade Range of Oregon and Washington, the Coast Ranges on the Pacific coastline, and the Sierra Nevada of California. These mountains are not shown on the map.

Mountain Ranges of the World

Monday

1. How many mountain ranges are shown on the map? Name the three that are in North or South America.

_____

_____

2. Name the labeled mountain ranges in Africa, Asia, and Europe.

_____

_____

Tuesday

1. Which mountain range is located in Africa? What is the name of the highest mountain in Africa, and where is it located?

_____

_____

2. The highest mountain in the world is located in Asia. Name the mountain and mountain range in which it stands.

_____

Wednesday

1. Which mountain range acts as a natural border between Europe and Asia?

_____

2. In Europe, the highest mountain is located in the Caucasus Mountains. Name this mountain.

_____

Mountain Ranges of the World

Thursday

1. North America has the Appalachians and the Rocky Mountains. It also has the Pacific Mountain System. Name at least three ranges in this system.

   _____

2. Which of the world's highest peaks stand apart from the mountain ranges labeled on this map?

   _____

   _____

Friday

1. What do these famous mountains have in common—Mount Etna in Sicily, Mount St. Helens in the U.S., and Mount Vesuvius in Italy?

   _____

2. Which mountain range, above or below sea level, is the longest in the world—the Andes, the Rocky Mountains, or the Mid-Atlantic Ridge?

   _____

Challenge

Fill out this chart on the highest mountains on the seven continents. The first one has been done for you. Use other references to help you with the others. Cut out the chart and attach it to the back of the map.

Mountain	Location	Height in Feet and Meters
1. Mount Everest	Nepal / Tibet border	29,035 ft./8,850 m
2. Aconcagua		
3. Mount McKinley		
4. Kilimanjaro		
5. Mount Elbrus		
6. Vinson Massif		
7. Mount Kosciuszko		

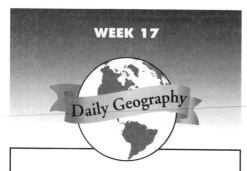

Deserts of the World

Introducing the Map

Explain to students that a physical map may show only one physical feature such as mountains or deserts. Share the following information about deserts with students as they look at the map of the deserts of the world:

- Deserts cover about a fifth of the Earth's land surface.

- Sand covers only about 10 to 20 percent of most deserts. The rest of the land is made of gravel-covered plains, hills and mountains, dry lake beds, and dry stream channels.

- Deserts are arid because they receive less than 10 inches (25 cm) of rain or snow each year.

- Sand seas cover large areas of the desert regions of Africa, Asia, and Australia.

- Most of the world's deserts are near the equator, so they are hot, but others are extremely cold. The temperature at the Gobi Desert in Asia can get as low as −40°F (−40°C).

- The largest hot desert in the world is the Sahara in northern Africa. The Sahara is roughly the size of the contiguous United States. Temperatures there can reach as high as 136°F (58°C).

- Wind and water erosion form buttes, mesas, and plateaus in deserts. Flash floods are sudden floods that occur when rain falls in a desert. The force of the water wears away the landscape.

- Polar regions are considered arid desert areas because nearly all the moisture is locked up in the form of ice.

Remind students that only a sampling of the deserts of the world are included on this map. Please note that the ecosystem of the Sahara Desert is included in Week 26.

Introducing Vocabulary

butte a flat-topped hill with steep sides; a column of rock

desert a dry region with little or no rainfall

dune a mound or ridge of windblown sand

mesa a flat-topped hill with steep sides; larger than a butte

oasis a place in the desert where there is a source of water and where plants grow

physical map a map that shows natural landforms and waterways on Earth's surface

plateau a flat-topped hill with steep sides; larger than a mesa

sand sea a vast region covered by sand and dunes

ANSWER KEY

Monday
1. Great Basin, Mohave, Sonoran, Chihuahuan, Patagonian, and Atacama
2. Sahara Desert; Africa

Tuesday
1. 6; Gobi Desert
2. Australian Desert

Wednesday
1. less than 10 inches of rain each year
2. Any four of the following: Arizona, California, Colorado, Nevada, New Mexico, Oregon, Texas, or Utah

Thursday
1. Arabian Desert
2. Atacama and Patagonian Deserts

Friday
1. 11
2. ⅕; 20%

Challenge
Gibson, Great Sandy, Great Victoria, and Simpson Deserts

Deserts of the World

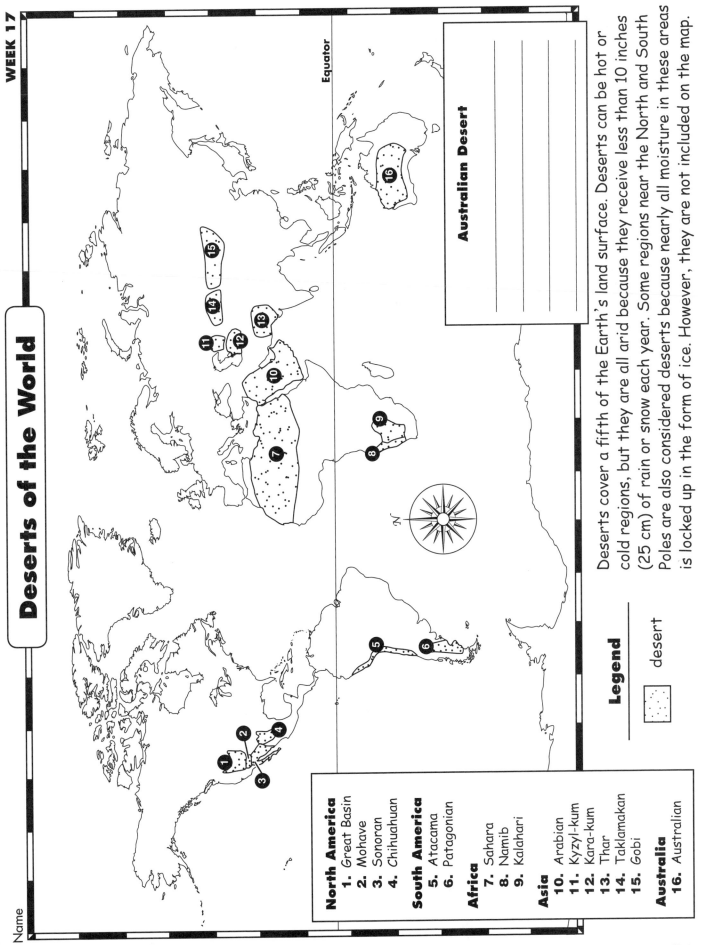

Australian Desert

Deserts cover a fifth of the Earth's land surface. Deserts can be hot or cold regions, but they are all arid because they receive less than 10 inches (25 cm) of rain or snow each year. Some regions near the North and South Poles are also considered deserts because nearly all moisture in these areas is locked up in the form of ice. However, they are not included on the map.

Legend

desert

Equator

North America
1. Great Basin
2. Mohave
3. Sonoran
4. Chihuahuan

South America
5. Atacama
6. Patagonian

Africa
7. Sahara
8. Namib
9. Kalahari

Asia
10. Arabian
11. Kyzyl-kum
12. Kara-kum
13. Thar
14. Taklamakan
15. Gobi

Australia
16. Australian

Name

Deserts of the World

Monday

1. Which deserts are located in the Western Hemisphere?

   _____

   _____

2. Which desert is the largest hot desert in the world? In which continent is it located?

   _____

Tuesday

1. How many deserts are located in Asia? Which desert is located the farthest east in the area of China?

   _____

   _____

2. Which desert is located on the smallest continent in the world?

   _____

Wednesday

1. Do most deserts receive, on average, less than 50 inches of rain, less than 10 inches of rain, or less than 1 inch of rain each year?

   _____

2. Name four states that would be included in at least one of the North American deserts.

   _____

   _____

Deserts of the World

Thursday

1. Name the Asian desert that borders Africa.

   _____

2. Which deserts are located in Chile and Argentina?

   _____

Friday

1. Of the 16 deserts on the map, how many are located north of the equator?

   _____

2. How much of Earth's land surface is desert? Write your answer as both a fraction and a percentage.

   fraction: _____   percentage: _____

Challenge

The Australian Desert actually consists of four deserts. Find out the names of these four deserts and add them to the list on the map. Use a reference physical map to help you.

Rivers of the World

Introducing the Map

Ask students to name as many rivers as they can. Students will probably name famous rivers like the Mississippi and the Nile. Tell students there are many famous rivers in the world. Share with students the following information as they look at the map of the rivers of the world:

- A river system includes the river and all the smaller streams that supply water to the river.

- A river is highest at its headwaters, or source, where it begins. It is lowest at its mouth, which is where it ends.

- Almost all river water comes from rain or melted snow. Most of the water reaches the river indirectly. Water called surface runoff flows over land to the river, or water soaks into the soil and becomes groundwater. The groundwater moves slowly through the ground to the rivers. Other sources of river water come from glaciers, springs, and overflowing lakes.

- Rivers are used for transportation, trade, agriculture, and as a source of power.

- The world's longest river is the Nile River in Africa. It is 4,160 miles (6,695 km) long.

- The Amazon River in South America is the second-longest river in the world. The Amazon has more water than any other river. It has more water than the Nile, the Mississippi, and the Yangtze combined.

- The third- and fifth-longest rivers are both in China—the Chang Jiang, or Yangtze, and the Huang He (Yellow) River.

- The Missouri River is the longest river of the U.S., but it is actually a tributary of the Mississippi River. The length of the combined Missouri-Mississippi River System is 3,740 miles long. That combined length would make the system the third-longest river in the world. The source of the Missouri is located in Montana, and then it flows into the Mississippi in Missouri. The Mississippi River's source is Lake Itasca in Minnesota, and the mouth of the river is the Mississippi delta in Louisiana, where it then flows into the Gulf of Mexico.

Remind students that only a sampling of the world's famous rivers are shown on this map.

Introducing Vocabulary

mouth the part of a river where it empties into another body of water

physical map a map that shows natural landforms and waterways on Earth's surface

river system a river and the smaller streams that supply water to the river

source the place where a river begins

tributary a smaller stream or river that flows into a larger one

---

WEEK 18

Daily Geography

ANSWER KEY

Monday
1. 8; Mackenzie and the Paraná Rivers
2. Mississippi River

Tuesday
1. Nile River
2. South America

Wednesday
1. Rio Grande
2. St. Lawrence River

Thursday
1. Huang He (Yellow) River
2. Volga River

Friday
1. Missouri-Mississippi River System
2. Lake Itasca in northern Minnesota is the source, and the mouth is located at the Mississippi delta in Louisiana, where it then flows into the Gulf of Mexico.

Challenge

River	Length
1. Nile	4,160 miles (6,695 km)
2. Amazon	4,000 miles (6,437 km)
3. Chang Jiang (Yangtze)	3,900 miles (6,276 km)
4. Yenisei River in Russia (not shown on map)	3,395 miles (5,464 km)

Name

Rivers of the World

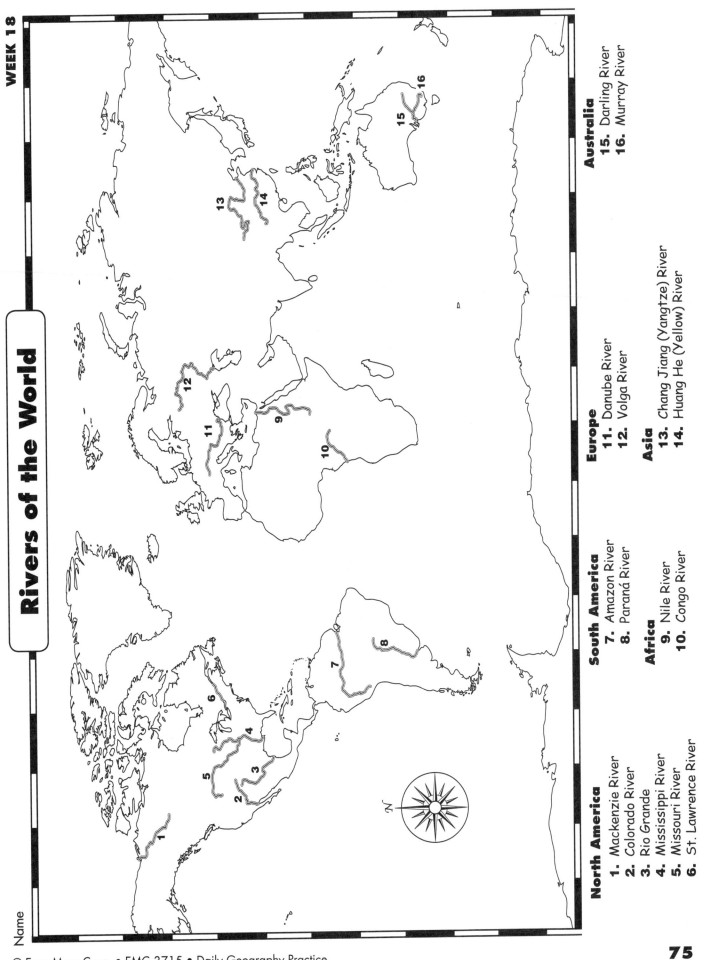

North America
1. Mackenzie River
2. Colorado River
3. Rio Grande
4. Mississippi River
5. Missouri River
6. St. Lawrence River

South America
7. Amazon River
8. Paraná River

Africa
9. Nile River
10. Congo River

Europe
11. Danube River
12. Volga River

Asia
13. Chang Jiang (Yangtze) River
14. Huang He (Yellow) River

Australia
15. Darling River
16. Murray River

Rivers of the World

Monday

1. How many rivers are labeled in the Western Hemisphere? Which river is the farthest north, and which river is the farthest south?

   _____

   _____

2. The longest river in the United States is the Missouri River. Which river is the second longest in the U.S.?

   _____

Tuesday

1. The world's longest river is located in Africa and is 4,160 miles (6,695 km) long. Name this famous river.

   _____

2. The world's second-longest river is the Amazon. In which continent is this 4,000-mile (6,437-km) river found?

   _____

Wednesday

1. Which river forms an international boundary between Mexico and the United States?

   _____

2. Name the river that links the Great Lakes and the Atlantic Ocean.

   _____

Rivers of the World

Thursday

1. The world's fifth-longest river has large amounts of yellow silt that is deposited along its course. Name this river.

   _____

2. Name the longest river in the European part of Russia.

   _____

Friday

1. Which river system in the United States can be called the third-longest river in the world?

   _____

2. Where are the source and the mouth of the Mississippi River located?

   _____

   _____

Challenge

Find out the length of the four longest rivers in the world. Write the figures in both miles and kilometers on the map. Use additional references to help you.

WEEK 19

Regions of the United States

Introducing the Map

Share with students that the United States is often divided into areas or regions. Each region has its own distinctive features. Similar physical features, climate, economy, traditions, and history define regions.

Show students the map of the United States. Look at the legend and identify the six regions. Then look at the Pacific region on the map. Ask students why Alaska, California, Hawaii, Oregon, and Washington are called the Pacific region. Students should recognize that all the states border the geographic feature of the Pacific Ocean. The Rocky Mountain region is also identified by its geographic features.

Look at other regions and discuss why they are called the Southwest, North-Central, Southeast, and Northeast. The students should conclude that those regions are generally based on directional locations.

Tell students that they will encounter other sources that name the regions differently. The North-Central states are also called the midwestern states on some maps, while the Southeast may just be called the southern states. Other sources will place states in different regions. For example, on some maps Arizona and New Mexico are included in the Rocky Mountain region. Delaware and Maryland are sometimes included in the Northeast region. Some sources divide regions into smaller regions. For example, the Northeast is divided into two smaller regions—New England and the Mid-Atlantic states.

This is also a good time for students to use their mental map skills since the states are not labeled, or you may choose to give students the U.S. map on page 7 as a reference. Here is a list of the states that belong to each region:

Pacific region (5 states): Alaska, California, Hawaii, Oregon, Washington

Rocky Mountain region (6 states): Colorado, Idaho, Montana, Nevada, Utah, Wyoming

Southwest region (4 states): Arizona, New Mexico, Oklahoma, Texas

North-Central region (12 states): Illinois, Indiana, Iowa, Kansas, Michigan, Minnesota, Missouri, Nebraska, North Dakota, Ohio, South Dakota, Wisconsin

Southeast region (14 states): Alabama, Arkansas, Delaware, Florida, Georgia, Kentucky, Louisiana, Maryland, Mississippi, North Carolina, South Carolina, Tennessee, Virginia, West Virginia

Northeast region (9 states): Connecticut, Maine, Massachusetts, New Hampshire, New Jersey, New York, Pennsylvania, Rhode Island, Vermont

Introducing Vocabulary

region an area of land or water with certain characteristics that make it different from other areas

---

ANSWER KEY

Monday
1. 6; Southeast region
2. Pacific region; They border the Pacific Ocean.

Tuesday
1. North-Central region
2. Rocky Mountain region; Colorado, Idaho, Montana, Nevada, Utah, and Wyoming

Wednesday
1. Arizona, California, New Mexico, and Texas
2. North-Central and Northeast regions and the countries of Canada and the United States

Thursday
1. 1. Southeast
   2. North-Central
   3. Northeast
   4. Rocky Mountain
   5. Pacific
   6. Southwest
2. Southwest region; Rocky Mountain region

Friday
1. Southeast region
2. 9; any three of the following: Connecticut, Maine, Massachusetts, New Hampshire, New Jersey, New York, Pennsylvania, Rhode Island, or Vermont

Challenge
See above for the names of the regions and states.

Name _____

Regions of the United States

Legend

Pacific

Rocky Mountain

Southwest

North-Central

Southeast

Northeast

ATLANTIC OCEAN

CANADA

GULF OF MEXICO

MEXICO

PACIFIC OCEAN

N

Regions of the United States

Monday

1. The United States is divided into how many regions? Which region includes the most states?

   _____

2. Alaska and Hawaii are part of which region? Why are they part of this region?

   _____

   _____

Tuesday

1. Which region could also be called the Midwest states?

   _____

2. Which region is named for a major landform? Which states belong to this region?

   _____

   _____

Wednesday

1. If a region were named the Mexican Border region, which states would be included?

   _____

2. The Great Lakes border two regions and two countries. Name them.

   _____

   _____

Regions of the United States

Thursday

1. Rank the six regions from largest to smallest based on the number of states in each region.

   _____

   _____

   _____

2. Arizona and New Mexico are in which region? Sometimes they are grouped with another region. In which region could they belong?

   _____

   _____

Friday

1. Washington, D.C., lies between Maryland and Virginia. In which region does the nation's capital belong?

   _____

2. How many states make up the Northeast region? Name at least three Northeast states.

   _____

   _____

Challenge

Make a chart listing the six regions. Under each region, list the states that belong to that region. Attach the chart to the map. Use a United States political map as a reference to help you name the states. Remember to make sure you include all 50!

The West Indies

Introducing the Map

Share with students the definition of a region. Discuss how each region has its own distinctive features. Similar physical features, climate, economy, traditions, and history can define different regions.

Show students the map of the West Indies. Share the following background information about this chain of islands while the students look at the map:

> The West Indies is a chain of islands that divide the Caribbean Sea from the rest of the Atlantic Ocean. The islands stretch about 2,000 miles (3,200 km) from southern Florida in the United States to the northern coast of Venezuela.

> The West Indies is made up of three major island groups. They are the Greater Antilles, the Lesser Antilles, and the Bahamas. The Bahamas consist of 3,000 small islands that are not geographically located in the Caribbean, but are included in the region. Thirteen independent countries and eleven dependencies make up this region.

> One similar feature of the region is the climate. The islands of the West Indies have a warm, tropical climate. Hurricanes frequently strike this region in late summer and early fall. There is also volcanic eruption activity in this region.

> Agriculture and tourism are the two major economic activities in this region. The region grows such products as bananas, cacao, citrus fruits, coffee, spices, sugar cane, and tobacco. More than 8 million people visit the islands each year because of the tropical climate, beautiful beaches, and lush scenery.

> The region can be identified historically. In 1492, Christopher Columbus became the first European to reach the islands when he landed on an island believed to be present-day San Salvador in the Bahamas. He called them the Indies because he believed they were the East Indies islands of Asia. The islands were later named the West Indies to distinguish them from the East Indies.

Introducing Vocabulary

dependency land and waters controlled by a state, nation, or government

Greater Antilles an island group of the West Indies including Cuba, Jamaica, Hispaniola (Dominican Republic and Haiti), and Puerto Rico (U.S.)

Lesser Antilles an island group of the West Indies including eight countries and eight dependencies

region an area of land or water with certain characteristics that make it different from other areas

West Indies an island chain that divides the Caribbean Sea from the rest of the Atlantic Ocean

---

ANSWER KEY

Monday
1. Caribbean Sea and Atlantic Ocean
2. Greater Antilles and Lesser Antilles

Tuesday
1. off the southeast coast of Florida
2. Cuba, Dominican Republic, Haiti, and Jamaica

Wednesday
1. 8 countries and 8 dependencies
2. Dominican Republic and Haiti

Thursday
1. Puerto Rico and the Virgin Islands
2. France, Netherlands, and the United Kingdom

Friday
1. Colombia, Mexico, United States, and Venezuela
2. Cuba; Greater Antilles

Challenge
In 1492, Christopher Columbus landed on San Salvador in the Bahamas. He called them the Indies because he thought he had landed in the East Indies of Asia. The islands were given the name West Indies to distinguish them from Asian islands.

The West Indies

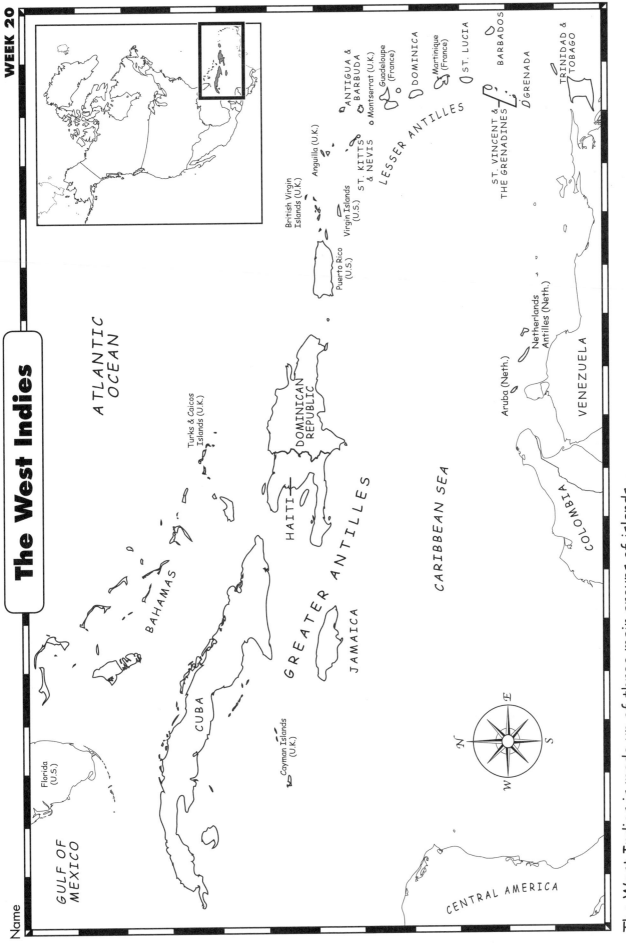

ATLANTIC OCEAN

GULF OF MEXICO

Florida (U.S.)

BAHAMAS

Turks & Caicos Islands (U.K.)

CUBA

Cayman Islands (U.K.)

JAMAICA

HAITI

DOMINICAN REPUBLIC

GREATER ANTILLES

CARIBBEAN SEA

British Virgin Islands (U.K.)

Puerto Rico (U.S.)

Virgin Islands (U.S.)

Anguilla (U.K.)

ST. KITTS & NEVIS

ANTIGUA & BARBUDA

Montserrat (U.K.)

Guadeloupe (France)

DOMINICA

Martinique (France)

ST. LUCIA

LESSER ANTILLES

ST. VINCENT & THE GRENADINES

BARBADOS

GRENADA

TRINIDAD & TOBAGO

Aruba (Neth.)

Netherlands Antilles (Neth.)

VENEZUELA

COLOMBIA

CENTRAL AMERICA

N E S W

The West Indies is made up of three main groups of islands— the Bahamas in the north, the Greater Antilles in the center, and the Lesser Antilles in the southeast. Thirteen countries and eleven dependencies are part of this region.

The West Indies

Monday

1. The West Indies is a chain of islands in which sea and ocean?

   _____

2. The West Indies is made up of the Bahamas and which two other island groups?

   _____

Tuesday

1. The Bahamas consist of 3,000 small islands. Where are the Bahamas located in relation to the United States?

   _____

2. Which four island nations make up the Greater Antilles?

   _____

   _____

Wednesday

1. How many countries and how many dependencies are located in the Lesser Antilles?

   _____

2. The island of Hispaniola consists of two nations in the Greater Antilles. Name the two countries that share this island.

   _____

The West Indies

Thursday

1. Which two dependencies in the West Indies belong to the United States?

   _____

2. Which European countries have dependencies in the West Indies?

   _____

   _____

Friday

1. Besides the five countries in Central America, which other countries border the West Indies?

   _____

   _____

2. Which island nation is the largest in area? Is it located in the Bahamas, the Greater Antilles, or the Lesser Antilles?

   _____

Challenge

Explain how the islands of the Bahamas, Greater Antilles, and Lesser Antilles got the name *West Indies*. Write your explanation as another caption for the map.

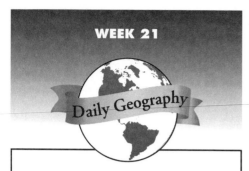

ANSWER KEY

Monday
1. 7; Belize, Costa Rica, Guatemala, Honduras, El Salvador, Nicaragua, and Panama
2. a narrow strip of land that connects two larger land areas

Tuesday
1. Caribbean Sea, Pacific Ocean, and the Gulfs of Fonseca, Honduras, Mosquitos, Nicoya, and Panama
2. Mexico and Colombia

Wednesday
1. Belize
2. Guatemala City, Panama City, and San Salvador

Thursday
1. El Salvador; Atlantic Ocean
2. Panama; Costa Rica, Colombia, the Pacific Ocean, and the Caribbean Sea

Friday
1. earthquakes, hurricanes, and volcanic eruptions
2. Greater Antilles

Challenge
The students should label the Panama Canal which runs across the center of the country of Panama, just above Panama City.

The Region of Central America

Introducing the Map

Review with students the definition of a region. Share with students that a group of countries can be part of a region, as learned in Week 20, or a country can have several regions, as learned in Week 19. Discuss how each region has its own distinctive features. Similar physical features, climate, economy, traditions, and history can define different regions.

Ask students to name the geographic region that bridges the southern end of North America to South America. The answer is the region of Central America.

Show students the map of Central America. Students should notice that the geographic location of this region gives it its name. However, remind students that Central America is considered part of the North American continent because it is north of the equator. Besides its geographic location, Central America is linked in other ways. Share the following information with students:

- The countries of Central America form a long isthmus that connects southern North America to South America. The Isthmus of Panama is a narrow strip of land that separates the Atlantic and Pacific Oceans in Panama.

- The physical features of the region include many inland, rugged mountains. Many of the mountains are active volcanoes. Devastating earthquakes, volcanic eruptions, and hurricanes strike this region.

- Spanish is the official language of all the Central American countries, except Belize. In Belize, English is the official language.

- Most of the people of Central America live in the highlands on small farms.

- Central America has large plantations that produce about 10 percent of the world's coffee and about 10 percent of the world's bananas.

- The Maya Indians were the dominant culture from about 400 B.C. to about A.D. 900. Today, descendants of the Maya live in the mountains of Central America.

All these factors help to group the countries into a region.

Introducing Vocabulary

Central America a region of seven countries between Mexico and South America including Belize, Costa Rica, El Salvador, Guatemala, Honduras, Nicaragua, and Panama

isthmus a narrow strip of land having water on each side and connecting two larger bodies of land

region an area of land or water with certain characteristics that make it different from other areas

MEXICO

BELIZE
⭐ Belmopan

GULF OF HONDURAS

CARIBBEAN SEA

GUATEMALA

Guatemala City ⭐

HONDURAS

Tegucigalpa ⭐

San Salvador ⭐

EL SALVADOR

GULF OF FONSECA

NICARAGUA

⭐ Managua

PACIFIC OCEAN

COSTA RICA

⭐ San José

GULF OF NICOYA

GULF OF MOSQUITOS

Panama City

SOUTH AMERICA

⭐

PANAMA

GULF OF PANAMA

COLOMBIA

N

Legend

⭐ national capital

The countries of Central America form a long isthmus between the rest of North America and the continent of South America.

The Region of Central America

Monday

1. How many countries make up the region of Central America? Name them.

   _____

   _____

2. Central America forms an isthmus between the southern part of North America and South America. What is an isthmus?

   _____

   _____

Tuesday

1. Which waterways border Central America?

   _____

   _____

2. Which countries border Central America to the north and south?

   _____

Wednesday

1. Which country does <u>not</u> border the Pacific Ocean?

   _____

2. Which capital cities are named after the countries' names?

   _____

The Region of Central America

Thursday

1. Which country does <u>not</u> border the Caribbean Sea? The Caribbean Sea flows into which ocean?

   _____

2. Which narrow country curves from the west to the east? Name its borders.

   _____

   _____

Friday

1. Because of its location, what three severe kinds of violent natural occurrences strike this region?

   _____

2. Look at the inset map. Is Central America closer to the Greater Antilles or to the Lesser Antilles?

   _____

Challenge

The Panama Canal is a waterway that cuts across the Isthmus of Panama. It links the Atlantic Ocean and the Pacific Ocean. The canal helps ships to travel between Atlantic and Pacific ports without sailing around South America.

On the map, label the Panama Canal. Use an atlas or other resource to help you with its location.

WEEK 22

Daily Geography

ANSWER KEY

Monday
1. 16 countries and
   3 continents
2. Africa and Europe

Tuesday
1. Egypt, Israel, Jordan, Saudi
   Arabia, and Yemen
2. Bahrain, Cyprus, Kuwait,
   Lebanon, and Qatar

Wednesday
1. Iran, Jordan, Kuwait, Saudi
   Arabia, Syria, and Turkey
2. Egypt and Israel

Thursday
1. Mediterranean Sea and
   the Red Sea
2. 7 countries

Friday
1. Gaza Strip and West Bank
2. Ancient Egypt and Ancient
   Mesopotamia (Sumer);
   Christianity, Islam, and
   Judaism

Challenge
1.	K	10.	L
2.	M	11.	H
3.	F	12.	N
4.	P	13.	G
5.	D	14.	C
6.	I	15.	A
7.	B	16.	O
8.	J		
9.	E		

The Middle East Region

Introducing the Map

Define the term *region*. Share with students that a group of countries can be part of a region. Discuss how each region has its own distinctive features. Similar physical features, climate, economy, ethnicity, history, language, religion, and traditions can define regions.

Tell students there is a large region that covers parts of northern Africa, southwestern Asia, and southeastern Europe. It is called the Middle East. Share with students that scholars disagree on which countries make up the Middle East. Many experts list the following sixteen countries that belong to the Middle East Region: Bahrain, Cyprus, Egypt, Iran, Iraq, Israel, Jordan, Kuwait, Lebanon, Oman, Qatar, Saudi Arabia, Syria, Turkey, United Arab Emirates, and Yemen.

Have students look at the map of the Middle East as you give them the following background information about this region:

- Two of the world's first civilizations—Ancient Egypt and Ancient Mesopotamia (Sumer)—developed in the Middle East region.

- The region is the birthplace of three major religions—Christianity, Judaism, and Islam. More than 90 percent of the people in the region are Muslims. Muslims are followers of Islam.

- Most of the people in the Middle East are Muslim Arabs. Other ethnic and religious groups are Black Africans, Armenians, Copts, Greeks, Iranians, Jews, Kurds, and Turks.

- The main language is Arabic. Persian (Farsi) is spoken in Iran, and people in Turkey speak Turkish. Most Israelis speak Hebrew.

- Oil production is a major industry. Major oil producers are Iran, Iraq, Kuwait, Oman, Qatar, Saudi Arabia, and the United Arab Emirates.

- The area including the State of Israel and the Arab territories of the Gaza Strip and the West Bank are historically known as Palestine. Conflict has plagued this region for centuries. Battles have been fought over land and resources. Both the State of Israel and the Palestinian Arabs in the Gaza Strip and the West Bank have clashed over rights to the land.

  Please note that this is a complicated situation. You may choose to discuss this issue in more detail or other issues like the Persian Gulf War, or other conflicts in this region.

Introducing Vocabulary

Middle East a large region that covers parts of northern Africa, southwestern Asia, and southeastern Europe

region an area of land or water with certain characteristics that make it different from other areas

THE MIDDLE EAST REGION

Name

LEGEND

——— international border

·········· disputed border

ASIA

EUROPE

CASPIAN SEA

STRAIT OF HORMUZ

GULF OF OMAN

ARABIAN SEA

IRAN

OMAN

INDIAN OCEAN

PERSIAN GULF

UNITED ARAB EMIRATES

BAHRAIN

QATAR

KUWAIT

YEMEN

IRAQ

SAUDI ARABIA

GULF OF ADEN

BLACK SEA

SYRIA

TURKEY

LEBANON

WEST BANK

ISRAEL

GAZA STRIP

JORDAN

SINAI PEN.

GULF OF AQABA

RED SEA

AFRICA

CYPRUS

SUEZ CANAL

MEDITERRANEAN SEA

EGYPT

AEGEAN SEA

EUROPE

N E W S

The Middle East Region

Monday

1. How many countries and continents make up the Middle East region?

   _____

2. The Middle East is usually considered part of Asia, but which other two continents have lands in the Middle East?

   _____

Tuesday

1. Which Middle East countries border the Red Sea?

   _____

   _____

2. Which five countries in the Middle East are the smallest in land area?

   _____

   _____

Wednesday

1. Which Middle East countries border Iraq?

   _____

   _____

2. The Sinai Peninsula joins which two Middle East countries?

   _____

   _____

The Middle East Region

Thursday

1. The Suez Canal on the Sinai Peninsula links which two bodies of water?

   _____

2. How many Middle East countries border the Persian Gulf?

   _____

Friday

1. Which two territories are within the boundaries of Israel?

   _____

2. Which two great ancient civilizations developed in the Middle East, and which three major religions were born in the region?

   _____

   _____

Challenge

Match the following capital cities to the countries in the Middle East. A few have been done for you. Cut and paste the quiz to the back of the Middle East map. Use a reference political map to help you.

1. __K__ Bahrain
2. _____ Cyprus
3. _____ Egypt
4. _____ Iran
5. _____ Iraq
6. _____ Israel
7. _____ Jordan
8. _____ Kuwait
9. _____ Lebanon

10. __L__ Oman
11. _____ Qatar
12. _____ Saudi Arabia
13. _____ Syria
14. _____ Turkey
15. __A__ United Arab Emirates
16. _____ Yemen

A. Abu Dhabi
B. Amman
C. Ankara
D. Baghdad
E. Beirut
F. Cairo
G. Damascus
H. Doha

I. Jerusalem
J. Kuwait City
K. Manama
L. Muscat
M. Nicosia
N. Riyadh
O. Sanaa
P. Tehran

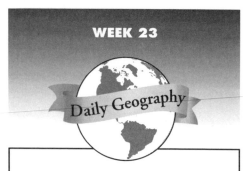

A National Symbol: Washington, D.C.

Introducing the Map

Ask students to name the capital of the United States. Students will name Washington, D.C. Explain that Washington covers the area of the District of Columbia, an area of land that is controlled by the federal government. It is the only American city that is not part of a state. Also, remind students that Washington is the headquarters of the country's national government. The president, members of Congress, and thousands of other government employees work there. Further explain that the city is a symbol for the country. It is a cultural landmark that stands for America's unity and democratic traditions.

Show students the map of Washington, D.C. Discuss the location of Washington, D.C. It lies on the Potomac River, between Maryland and Virginia.

The map shows points of interest in west-central Washington. Tell students that there are over 80 important buildings in this area, but the map shows only a sampling of the many popular tourist attractions.

Have students locate the White House on the map. Tell them that the president has the most famous address in the United States—1600 Pennsylvania Avenue. Locate other buildings on the map with the students.

Introducing Vocabulary

capital a city in a country or state where the government is based

Capitol the building in Washington, D.C., occupied by the Congress of the U.S.

Capitol Hill the hill in Washington, D.C., on which stands the Capitol building

cultural landmark a place selected and pointed out as important to a group of people

District of Columbia (D.C.) an area of land controlled by the federal government

Ellipse an oval-shaped, park-like area in Washington, D.C.

memorial something built to honor a person or an event, such as a monument or a statue

National Mall a public walkway in Washington, D.C.

ANSWER KEY

Monday
1. District of Columbia
2. Maryland and Virginia

Tuesday
1. White House; 1600 Pennsylvania Avenue
2. Any four of the following: National Museum of American History, National Museum of Natural History, National Air and Space Museum, National Gallery of Art, and the Hirshhorn Museum

Wednesday
1. U.S. Capitol and the Washington Monument
2. park-like area between the White House and the Washington Monument

Thursday
1. Vietnam Veterans Memorial
2. Library of Congress, Supreme Court, and the U.S. Capitol

Friday
1. Jefferson and Lincoln Memorials, and the Washington Monument; all were presidents
2. the National Archives

Challenge
Students should write a caption on the map page using ideas such as: It is the nation's capital; it is home to the national government and its leaders; or that its famous buildings and memorials bring a sense of pride to the country.

Name

A National Symbol: Washington, D.C.

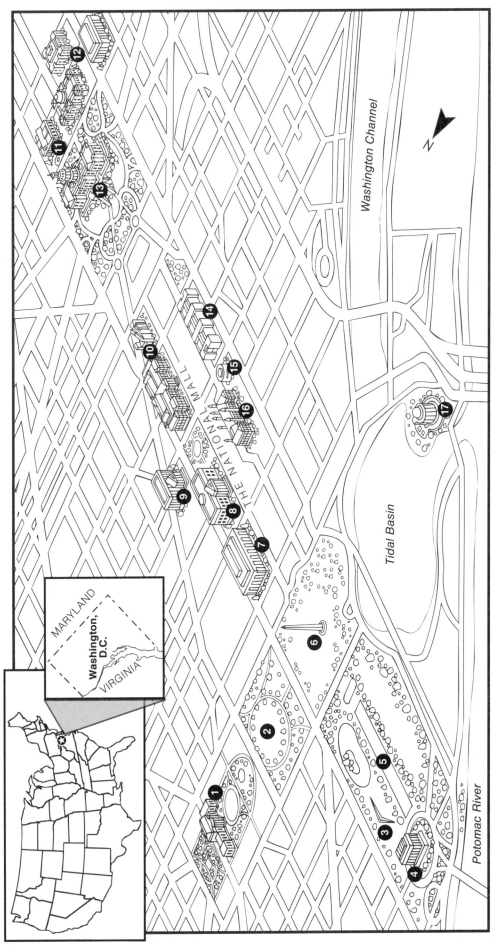

1. White House
2. The Ellipse
3. Vietnam Veterans Memorial
4. Lincoln Memorial
5. Reflecting Pool
6. Washington Monument

7. National Museum of American History
8. National Museum of Natural History
9. National Archives
10. National Gallery of Art
11. Supreme Court
12. Library of Congress

13. U.S. Capitol
14. National Air and Space Museum
15. Hirshhorn Museum
16. Smithsonian Institution
17. Jefferson Memorial

A National Symbol: Washington, D.C.

Monday

1. What do the initials *D.C.* stand for in Washington, D.C.?

   _____

2. Washington, D.C., is located between which two states?

   _____

Tuesday

1. The president of the U.S. lives and works in which building? What is the address of this building?

   _____

2. The Smithsonian Institution is the headquarters for many museums. Name four labeled museums on the National Mall.

   _____

   _____

Wednesday

1. The National Mall is a park-like area. Which two buildings act as the east-west borders for the Mall?

   _____

2. What is the Ellipse, and which two buildings flank this area?

   _____

   _____

A National Symbol:
Washington, D.C.

Thursday

1. Which labeled memorial honors veterans of a war?

   _____

   _____

2. Capitol Hill rises 88 feet (27 m). Which three important labeled
   government buildings stand on the hill?

   _____

   _____

Friday

1. Name three labeled memorials that honor a famous person. Why are
   these people being honored?

   _____

   _____

   _____

2. Two historic documents—the Constitution and the Declaration of
   Independence—are archived in which building?

   _____

Challenge

Washington, D.C., is called a national symbol, or a cultural landmark, for the
country. Why? Write your answer on the back of the map.

WEEK 24

National Parks of Utah

Introducing the Map

Tell students that places, buildings, structures, and statues have come to represent or symbolize a region. Give students the example of Washington, D.C. When people think of the nation's capital, famous buildings such as the White House, Washington Memorial, or the Lincoln Memorial come to mind. Ask students to name some other cultural symbols in the United States. They may come up with such symbols or national monuments as the Statue of Liberty, Mount Rushmore, or the Gateway Arch in St. Louis.

Share with students that cultural landmarks can also include places such as national parks. National parks serve important purposes such as appreciation of nature, recreational use, tourism, education, and the preservation of cultural and historical heritage.

Further explain that the National Park Service is a bureau of the United States Department of the Interior. It manages the 55 national parks in the United States. Most of the national parks are preserved mainly for their outstanding natural beauty or for the scientific importance of their physical features. The parklands are to be left undisturbed as much as possible. That includes the plants and animals of the area. Fishing is allowed, but hunting, lumbering, and mining are prohibited in most areas.

Show students the map of Utah. Students will notice there are five national parks in this state. They are Arches, Bryce Canyon, Capitol Reef, Canyonlands, and Zion National Parks. Read the information about each of the parks and talk about why it is important to preserve and protect these national parks.

Introducing Vocabulary

cultural landmark a place selected and pointed out as important to a group of people

national park an area set aside by a nation's government to protect natural beauty, wildlife, or other remarkable features

ANSWER KEY

Monday
1. 5; southern
2. Capitol Reef; The name comes from the fact that a long ridge is topped by white sandstone that looks like a capitol dome.

Tuesday
1. Arches and Canyonlands; Arches has 2,000 sandstone arches, and Canyonlands has a series of canyons called the Maze.
2. castles, cathedrals, and wild animals

Wednesday
1. Arches, Canyonlands, and Capitol Reef
2. Colorado and Green Rivers

Thursday
1. Great Basin (desert), lakes, mountains, plateau, and rivers
2. Fremont Indians left petroglyphs, which are drawings, on the cliff walls.

Friday
1. The lands have been set aside by the federal government for the preservation and appreciation of nature.
2. Zion National Park

Challenge
Students should write one or two facts about Rainbow Bridge on the map page. Examples of facts: Rainbow Bridge is the world's largest natural bridge. It is nearly 290 feet from its base to the top of the arch. The top of the arch is 42 feet thick and 33 feet wide.

Name

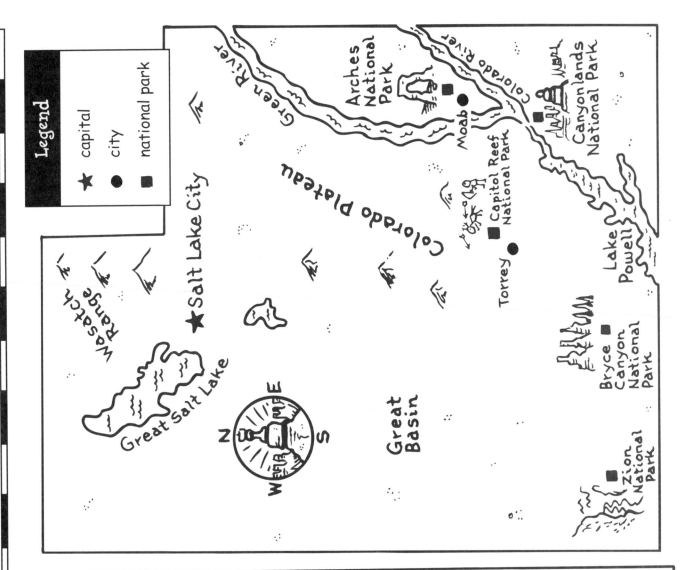

© Evan-Moor Corp. • EMC 3715 • Daily Geography Practice

National Parks of Utah

Arches National Park has over 2,000 sandstone arches. Landscape Arch is one of the world's longest natural arches. It is 291 feet (89 m) long.

Bryce Canyon National Park contains unusual rock formations that are in more than 60 shades of copper, cream, pink, and red. Rocks are in the shapes of castles, cathedrals, and even wild animals.

Canyonlands National Park is noted for its red rock canyons, sandstone spires, and a series of canyons called the Maze.

Capitol Reef National Park is famous for its long ridge that is topped by white sandstone that looks like a capitol dome. Petroglyphs and pictographs left by the Fremont Indians can be seen on cliff walls.

Zion National Park is known for its steep and narrow canyons and its unusual rock formations. Zion Canyon in the park is about 10 miles (16 km) long. Its walls reach 3,000 feet (910 m) high in some places.

Rainbow Bridge _____

_____

National Parks of Utah

Monday

1. How many national parks are in Utah? Are they located in the northern or the southern part of the state?

_____

2. Which national park is near Torrey? How did it get its name?

_____

_____

Tuesday

1. Which national parks are near Moab? How did they get their names?

_____

_____

2. Bryce Canyon National Park has unusual rock formations. The rocks are in which unusual shapes?

_____

_____

Wednesday

1. Which national parks are southeast of the state's capital city?

_____

2. Which two rivers are near or in two national parks?

_____

National Parks of Utah

Thursday

1. Besides canyons, what other physical features are shown on the map of Utah?

   _____

2. How can historians tell that native peoples made their home in the Capitol Reef National Park area?

   _____

Friday

1. National parks are considered cultural landmarks. Why?

   _____

2. Which park contains a canyon that is 10 miles (16 km) long with walls that reach 3,000 feet (910 m) high?

   _____

   _____

Challenge

Besides the five national parks, Utah has many national monuments. One of the most famous is called Rainbow Bridge National Monument. It is the world's largest natural rock bridge. It is in the shape of an arch. From its base to the top of the arch is 290 feet (88 m). The top of the arch is 42 feet (13 m) thick and 33 feet (10 m) wide.

Write one or two facts about Rainbow Bridge on the map and add a picture of the bridge to the map. Rainbow Bridge is located southeast of Lake Powell. You may wish to use additional resources to find out more about Rainbow Bridge.

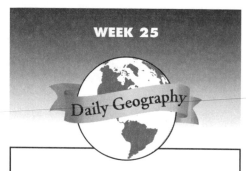

WEEK 25

Climate Zones of the United States

Introducing the Map

Ask students to describe the weather today in their area. Words such as *sunny and warm*, or *cool and rainy* will probably be mentioned. Explain that weather is the day-to-day change in the atmosphere around them. Tell students that the three most important elements that make up weather are precipitation, temperature, and wind.

Then discuss the climate in their area. Explain that climate is the usual weather in an area over a long period of time. Some words that describe climates are *arctic, temperate,* and *tropical.*

Show students the map of the climate zones. Have students find their state on the map. Then look at the legend to find the climate that is typical in their area of the United States. There may be more than one zone in their area. Go over the map legend carefully so that students understand the different climate zones of the country.

Explain to students the phrase "temperatures and precipitation vary with altitude." Altitude is the height above sea level. Unpredictable and extreme weather patterns happen at very low altitudes (deserts) and at very high altitudes (mountains). Define other words that may be unfamiliar to the students such as *arid, humid, latitude,* and *moderate,* as well as the vocabulary list given below.

Introducing Vocabulary

arctic climate a climate of extreme cold

climate usual weather in a particular place over a period of time

climate zone a region in which usual weather patterns occur over time

precipitation rain, snow, sleet, hail, or drizzle

temperate climate a climate without extremes of either cold or heat

tropical climate a climate of heat and rain

weather conditions in the Earth's atmosphere at a certain place and time

---

ANSWER KEY

Monday
1. 10
2. Tropical and Tundra Zones

Tuesday
1. Florida and Hawaii; Florida's southern tip is in the Tropical Zone, and all of the Hawaiian Islands are in the Tropical Zone.
2. Subarctic and Tundra Climate Zones

Wednesday
1. Continental moist; Any three of the following: Illinois, Indiana, Michigan, Minnesota, Ohio, Pennsylvania, New York, or Wisconsin
2. Humid subtropical; Florida and West Virginia

Thursday
1. California; Desert, Highland, Marine, Mediterranean, and Semiarid
2. Arizona, California, Nevada, New Mexico, Texas, and Utah

Friday
1. Alaska, Arizona, California, Nevada, New Mexico, Oregon, Texas, Utah, and Washington
2. Desert, Semiarid, and Tundra Climate Zones

Challenge
Students should color their state and list the climate zone(s) in which they live. They should also include an explanation of the typical climate conditions of their state.

Name _____

Climate Zones of the United States

Legend

Tropical—Warm throughout the year; light to heavy precipitation

Desert—Dry; temperature varies with altitude and latitude

Semiarid—Temperature varies with altitude and latitude; light precipitation

Mediterranean—Hot, dry summers; mild winters with moderate precipitation

Marine—Warm summers; cool winters; moderate precipitation

Humid subtropical—Hot summers; cool winters; moderate precipitation

Continental moist—Mild summers; cold winters; moderate precipitation

Highland—Temperatures and precipitation vary with altitude

Subarctic—Cold winters; cool summers; precipitation in summer

Tundra—Always cold; little precipitation

N

Climate Zones of the United States

Monday

1. How many different kinds of climate zones are shown on the map?

   _____

2. Which two climate zones are the direct opposites—one is always warm and one is always cold?

   _____

Tuesday

1. Which states include tropical climates? Which part of each state includes the Tropical Climate Zone?

   _____

   _____

2. Alaska is unique. It includes two climate zones that are not found in any other state. What are they?

   _____

Wednesday

1. The states that border the Great Lakes are in which climate zone? Name three states that border the Great Lakes.

   _____

   _____

2. In which climate zone does almost all of the Southeast region belong? Which states are the exception in the Southeast?

   _____

Climate Zones of the United States

Thursday

1. Which state has five climate zones? Name the climate zones.

   _____

   _____

2. Which states are in the Desert Climate Zone?

   _____

   _____

Friday

1. Which states have more than two climate zones within their borders?

   _____

   _____

   _____

2. Which three climate zones have the least amount of precipitation?

   _____

   _____

Challenge

Color your state on the map page. Write a caption for the map, explaining the climate zone or zones in your state.

The Sahara Desert

Introducing the Map

Define a biome and an ecosystem for students. Talk about different biomes in the world such as deserts, grasslands, tundra, and tropical rainforests.

Tell students that the Sahara Desert is one of the largest ecosystems in the world. It is also the largest desert in the world. Show students the map of the Sahara Desert and read about the kinds of animals and plants that live in the desert. Also, share the following interesting facts about the Sahara Desert:

ANSWER KEY

Monday
1. Red Sea
2. roughly equal to the size of the U.S.

Tuesday
1. oases and rivers
2. Nile River

Wednesday
1. a place in the desert where there is a source of water
2. vast seas of sand

Thursday
1. Any two of the following: Some plants are short-lived. Their seeds lie in the ground until it rains. Their life cycle is six to eight weeks. Some have long roots that reach deep into the soil. Others take moisture from the air through their leaves.
2. Any two of the following: They can go long periods without water. They get water from the plants they eat. They hunt for food at night when it is cooler.

Friday
1. Many are nomadic herders who travel seasonally to find water and pastures for their animals. They live in the oases where water and plants can be found.
2. A community of animals and plants interact and adapt to the Sahara's physical environment.

Challenge
Algeria, Chad, Egypt, Libya, Mali, Mauritania, Morocco, Niger, Sudan, Tunisia, and the Western Sahara (occupied by Morocco)

- The Sahara covers about 3½ million square miles (9 mil. sq. km). The desert covers parts of ten countries in Africa.

- It is covered by mountains, rocky areas, gravel plains, and salt flats. In addition, there are huge seas of sand, called ergs, which lie in large basins. The ergs form sand dunes as high as 600 feet (180 m).

- The Sahara has about 90 large oases and many small oases.

- The Sahara has a hot, dry climate. The annual rainfall averages less than 4 inches (10 cm). Daily summer temperatures average above 90°F (32°C). The highest recorded temperature is 136°F (58°C). Daily winter temperatures average from 50 to 60°F (10 to 16°C).

- Most of the two million people that live in the desert are nomads who tend herds of camels, cattle, goats, and sheep. They live in the oasis areas and travel seasonally to find available water sources and pastures for their animals. The Saharan people mainly use camels for transportation in the desert.

Please note that a sampling of the animals and plants that live in the Sahara are listed on the map page.

Introducing Vocabulary

biome a large area or environment that shares the same general climate of temperature and rainfall; different biomes support different types of plants and animals

desert a dry region with little or no rainfall

dune a mound or ridge of windblown sand

ecosystem a community of animals and plants interacting with their environment

erg a vast sea of sand

nomad a person who moves from place to place looking for food, water, and grazing land for his livestock

oasis a place in the desert where there is a source of water and where plants grow

sand sea a vast region covered by sand and dunes

The Sahara Desert

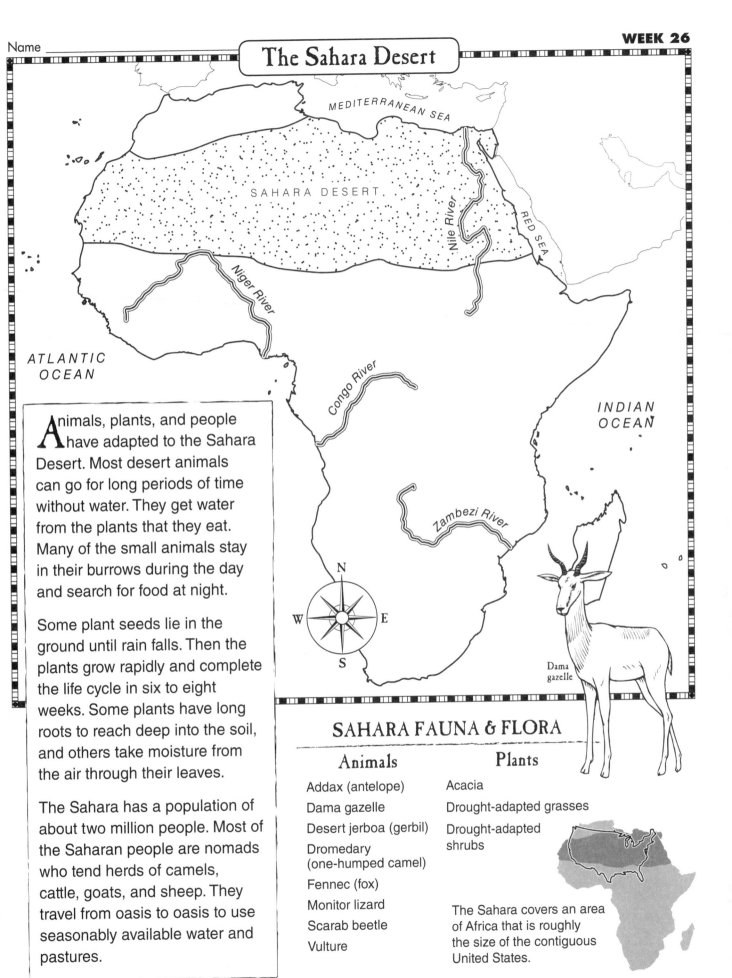

MEDITERRANEAN SEA

SAHARA DESERT

Nile River

RED SEA

Niger River

ATLANTIC OCEAN

Congo River

INDIAN OCEAN

Zambezi River

N
W E
S

Dama gazelle

Animals, plants, and people have adapted to the Sahara Desert. Most desert animals can go for long periods of time without water. They get water from the plants that they eat. Many of the small animals stay in their burrows during the day and search for food at night.

Some plant seeds lie in the ground until rain falls. Then the plants grow rapidly and complete the life cycle in six to eight weeks. Some plants have long roots to reach deep into the soil, and others take moisture from the air through their leaves.

The Sahara has a population of about two million people. Most of the Saharan people are nomads who tend herds of camels, cattle, goats, and sheep. They travel from oasis to oasis to use seasonably available water and pastures.

SAHARA FAUNA & FLORA

Animals

Addax (antelope)

Dama gazelle

Desert jerboa (gerbil)

Dromedary (one-humped camel)

Fennec (fox)

Monitor lizard

Scarab beetle

Vulture

Plants

Acacia

Drought-adapted grasses

Drought-adapted shrubs

The Sahara covers an area of Africa that is roughly the size of the contiguous United States.

The Sahara Desert

Monday

1. The Sahara Desert covers northern Africa from the Atlantic Ocean to which sea?

   _____

2. The Sahara Desert covers 3½ million square miles. Does that mean it is much smaller, roughly equal to, or much larger than the U.S.?

   _____

Tuesday

1. Which two physical features help to make parts of the Sahara Desert more livable?

   _____

2. Which river flows through the northeastern edge of the Sahara Desert?

   _____

Wednesday

1. The Sahara has about 90 large oases. What is an oasis?

   _____

2. The Sahara is covered by rocky plateaus, gravel plains, and ergs. What are ergs?

   _____

Daily Geography

The Sahara Desert

Thursday

1. Name two ways plants have adapted to the landscape of the Sahara.

   _____

   _____

2. Name two ways animals have adapted to the harsh environment of the Sahara.

   _____

   _____

Friday

1. Name two ways in which most people have adapted to living in the Sahara Desert.

   _____

   _____

2. The Sahara Desert is considered an ecosystem. Why?

   _____

   _____

Challenge

The Sahara Desert covers parts of ten countries and one occupied territory in northern Africa. List the countries and territory on the back of the map. Use an atlas, encyclopedia, or other resource to help you.

World's Ten Most Populous Countries

Introducing the Map

Ask students if they know the population of their city, state, or country. Tell students there is a national government agency that collects population information. It is called The Bureau of the Census, which is an agency of the Department of Commerce. The Census Bureau conducts censuses of population, housing, and other areas. The bureau gathers population data such as the total number of people and their ages, education, employment, income, marital status, race, and sex.

Tell students that within the U.S. Census Bureau there is an International Programs Center, which keeps an international data base. The International Data Base (IDB) is a computerized source of demographic and socioeconomic statistics for all the countries and areas of the world. The IDB combines data from country sources like censuses and surveys. International Programs Center personnel then analyze the information. They provide population information dating back as far as 1950 and as far ahead as 2050. There is also a World POPClock that gives an up-to-the-second simulation of the current world population.

Have students look at the world map and chart of the ten most populous countries in the world for 2010. Remind students that these statistics change yearly since population trends fluctuate. As a class, you may choose to go to the Internet site for the U.S. Census Bureau (www.census.gov) to look at current statistics and to look at the World POPClock site.

Introducing Vocabulary

census an official count of all the people living in a country or district

population (populous) total number of people who live in a place

statistics a fact or piece of information expressed as a number or percentage

ANSWER KEY

Monday
1. U.S. Census Bureau; 2010
2. China; billions

Tuesday
1. 308,282,053
2. Asia

Wednesday
1. Brazil; South America
2. 5; China, India, U.S., Indonesia, and Brazil

Thursday
1. China's population minus Japan's population is 1,202,562,150
2. 9

Friday
1. Antarctica and Australia; Russia covers large parts of Asia and Europe, so technically only two continents are correct.
2. India and the United States

Challenge
Students should add the following information to the map page:

11.	Mexico	112,468,855
12.	Philippines	99,900,177
13.	Vietnam	89,571,130
14.	Ethiopia	88,013,491
15.	Germany	81,644,454

World's Ten Most Populous Countries

Name

Countries Ranked by Population: 2010

	Country	Population
1.	China	1,330,141,295
2.	India	1,173,108,018
3.	United States	308,282,053
4.	Indonesia	242,968,342
5.	Brazil	201,103,330
6.	Pakistan	184,404,791
7.	Nigeria	161,604,744
8.	Bangladesh	156,118,464
9.	Russia	139,390,205
10.	Japan	127,579,145

World's Population Over Time

1950	2,555,360,972
2000	6,079,006,982
2050	9,084,495,405 (projected)

Source: U.S. Census Bureau, International Data Base

World's Ten Most Populous Countries

Monday

1. The population statistics on the map and chart are from which government agency? The statistics are from which year?

   _____

2. In 2010, which country was the most populous in the world? Is the population of that country in the millions, billions, or trillions?

   _____

Tuesday

1. What was the population of the United States in 2010?

   _____

2. Which continent has the most countries in the "top ten list"?

   _____

Wednesday

1. Which country had a population of just over 200 million in 2010? In which continent is this country located?

   _____

2. How many countries had a population of over 200 million in 2010? Name them.

   _____

   _____

World's Ten Most Populous Countries

Thursday

1. What was the difference in population between the most populous and the least populous countries on the list?

   _____

2. The world's population went over 6 billion in 1999. The estimate for the world's population in 2050 is over ___ billion.

Friday

1. Which continents do not have any of the top ten most populous countries in the world?

   _____

2. Which group of countries had a larger combined population—China and Japan, or India and the U.S.?

   _____

Challenge

Which five countries would round out the top fifteen most populous countries for 2010? What are their populations? Add the five countries and their populations to the map. Use the U.S. Census Bureau information to help you find your answers.

WEEK 28

Daily Geography

A Cultural Map: National Basketball Association

Introducing the Map

Survey the students to find out how many watch professional basketball. Ask students to name as many National Basketball Association (NBA) teams as they can. Students will probably be able to name quite a few, but will they be able to locate them on a map?

Share with students that a cultural map can show them just that. Discuss the kinds of things that are shown on a cultural map. Then show students the map of the United States and part of Canada. They should recognize that this is a cultural map, since it focuses on a recreational pastime of many people. The map shows the location of the NBA teams in North America. The NBA consists of 30 teams divided into two conferences—the Eastern and the Western. In the Eastern Conference, there are 15 teams. The fifteen teams are divided into three divisions—Atlantic (5 teams), Central (5 teams), and Southeast (5 teams). In the Western Conference, there are 15 teams. The 15 teams are divided into three divisions—Northwest (5 teams), Southwest (5 teams), and Pacific (5 teams).

Each team plays an 82-game schedule. After the regular season ends, the eight teams in each conference with the best records qualify for the playoffs. The playoffs first determine the conference champions. The conference champions then meet in a best-of-seven series for the league championship.

Read the list of teams in the index. Tell students the teams are listed in alphabetical order. Have students notice that the numbers on the index correspond to the numbers on the map. Most teams are named after the city in which they play. Several are not, so the cities in which they play are included in parentheses.

The state names are not given on the map, so students will have to use their mental map skills. You may choose to give students a political map of the United States for reference. You may also want to research which teams belong to which conference and division for further study.

Introducing Vocabulary

cultural map a map that shows patterns of ethnic groups, religious practices, languages spoken, educational levels, and recreational choices

culture language, beliefs, traditions, arts and crafts, political systems, and technologies of a group of people

ANSWER KEY

Monday
1. 29 in the U.S. and 1 in Canada
2. Toronto Raptors

Tuesday
1. eastern
2. 4; Golden State Warriors, Los Angeles Clippers, Los Angeles Lakers, and the Sacramento Kings

Wednesday
1. Texas; Dallas Mavericks
2. 1; Portland Trail Blazers

Thursday
1. Chicago, IL; Los Angeles, CA; Houston, TX; and San Antonio, TX
2. 6; Chicago Bulls, Cleveland Cavaliers, Indiana Pacers, Milwaukee Bucks, Minnesota Timberwolves, and Detroit Pistons

Friday
1. Any four of the following: Boston Celtics, Brooklyn Nets, New York Knicks, Philadelphia 76ers, and the Toronto Raptors
2. Any four of the following: Golden State Warriors, Los Angeles Clippers, Los Angeles Lakers, Phoenix Suns, and the Sacramento Kings

Challenge
Answers will vary.

A Cultural Map

National Basketball
Association

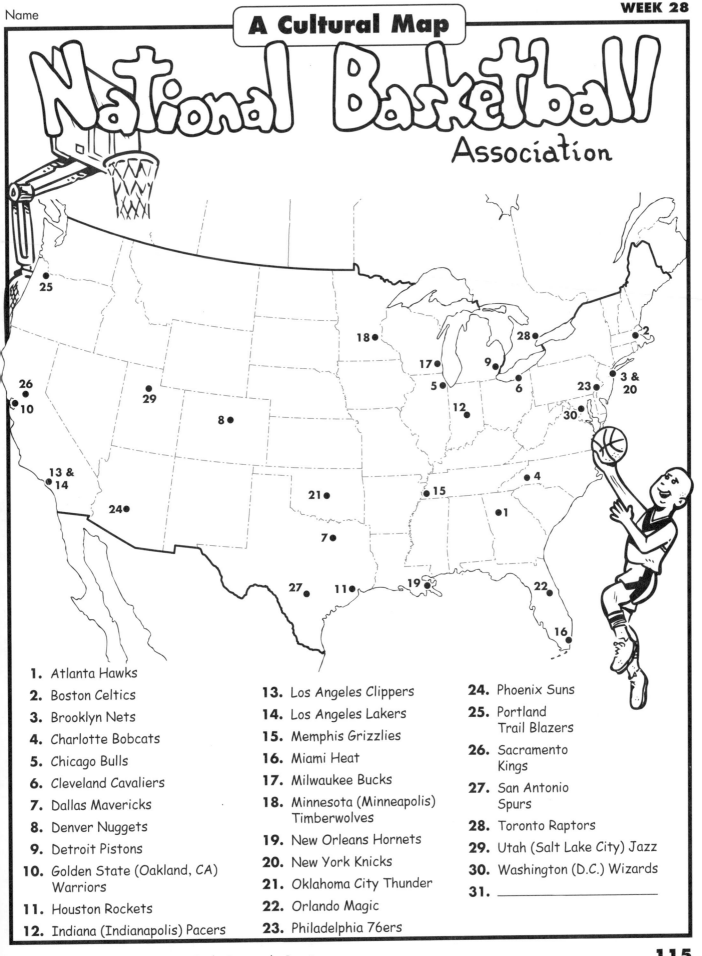

1. Atlanta Hawks
2. Boston Celtics
3. Brooklyn Nets
4. Charlotte Bobcats
5. Chicago Bulls
6. Cleveland Cavaliers
7. Dallas Mavericks
8. Denver Nuggets
9. Detroit Pistons
10. Golden State (Oakland, CA) Warriors
11. Houston Rockets
12. Indiana (Indianapolis) Pacers

13. Los Angeles Clippers
14. Los Angeles Lakers
15. Memphis Grizzlies
16. Miami Heat
17. Milwaukee Bucks
18. Minnesota (Minneapolis) Timberwolves
19. New Orleans Hornets
20. New York Knicks
21. Oklahoma City Thunder
22. Orlando Magic
23. Philadelphia 76ers

24. Phoenix Suns
25. Portland Trail Blazers
26. Sacramento Kings
27. San Antonio Spurs
28. Toronto Raptors
29. Utah (Salt Lake City) Jazz
30. Washington (D.C.) Wizards
31. _____

A Cultural Map:
National Basketball Association

Monday

1. How many NBA teams are located in the U.S., and how many are located in Canada?

   _____

2. What is the name of the NBA team in Canada?

   _____

Tuesday

1. Are most of the NBA teams located in the eastern or western part of the United States?

   _____

2. How many NBA teams are located in California? Name them.

   _____

   _____

Wednesday

1. Which state is home to the Mavericks, Rockets, and Spurs? Which team is located in the northeastern part of the state?

   _____

2. How many teams are located in the Pacific Northwest? Name them.

   _____

   _____

A Cultural Map:
National Basketball Association

Thursday

1. Since 1990, the Bulls, Lakers, and Spurs have each been an NBA champion at least four times. Where are these teams located?

   _____

   _____

2. How many NBA teams are located in the North-Central region of the United States? Name them.

   _____

   _____

Friday

1. Name 4 of the 5 NBA teams that are in the Eastern Conference, Atlantic Division.

   _____

   _____

2. Name 4 of the 5 NBA teams that are in the Western Conference, Pacific Division.

   _____

   _____

Challenge

Pretend you have just been appointed to name the next NBA team. Choose which city and state you think should have one. Name the NBA team. Place a dot on the map on the location of the new team. Add the team to the index at the bottom of the page.

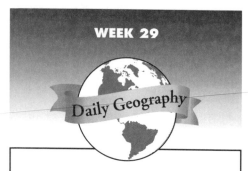
Skill: Economics

Essential Element 4: Standard 11

Leading Rice-Producing Countries

Introducing the Map

Ask students to name the world's most important food crops or staples of life. Tell students that almost everyone in the world eats one of the five staples of life—corn (maize), cassava (starchy root), potatoes, rice, or wheat. More than half the people in the world eat rice as the main part of their meals. Nearly all the people who depend on rice for food live on the continent of Asia.

Show students the map of the five leading rice-growing countries in the world. They should notice that the top producers of rice are all located in Asia. Share the following facts about rice as the students study the map:

- Scientists have identified 20 species of rice, but only two are cultivated today—Asian rice and African rice. Nearly all rice that is cultivated is Asian rice.

- Farmers grow rice in more than 100 countries, but Asian farmers grow about 90 percent of the world's rice. China and India produce more than half of the world's rice.

- Agriculture has been the main economic activity in China for thousands of years. About 60 percent of all workers in China are farmers. Nearly all of China's cropland is in the eastern half of the country. In southern China, rice, sweet potatoes, and tea are major crops. Wheat is the chief crop in the north.

- Rice grows best when there is an average temperature of at least 70°F (21°C) and with a yearly rainfall of at least 40 inches (100 cm).

- Rice grows best in a field covered with shallow water. Farmers build dikes or levees in lowlands and flood the fields to make rice paddies. Rice farming is mostly done by hand. Seedlings are transplanted from beds into flooded fields. At harvest time, farmers cut the rice stalks and place them into bundles to dry. The dried stalks are then beaten against screens to separate the grain.

Introducing Vocabulary

agriculture the business of farming

economy the way a state or country develops, distributes, and uses its money, goods, and services

product a material that is manufactured or refined for sale; an economic good

rice paddy a rice field

staple a basic food that is always produced and sold

ANSWER KEY

Monday
1. the top five rice-producing countries, which are all in Asia; metric tons of rice produced in each country
2. Eastern half of Asia, especially central and southeast Asia

Tuesday
1. China; 130 million metric tons
2. China and India

Wednesday
1. India, Indonesia, and Bangladesh produce about 170 million metric tons of rice, which is 20 million more than China and Vietnam.
2. Japan, Myanmar (formally Burma), Philippines, and Thailand

Thursday
1. warm temperatures (averages at least 70°F) and plenty of rainfall (averages at least 40 inches of rain each year)
2. 90 percent

Friday
1. They build dikes or levees and flood fields to make rice paddies.
2. Rice is a basic food that is a major part of the diet for over half of the world's population.

Challenge
The top six rice-producing states in the U.S. are Arkansas, California, Louisiana, Mississippi, Missouri, and Texas.

Leading Rice-Producing Countries

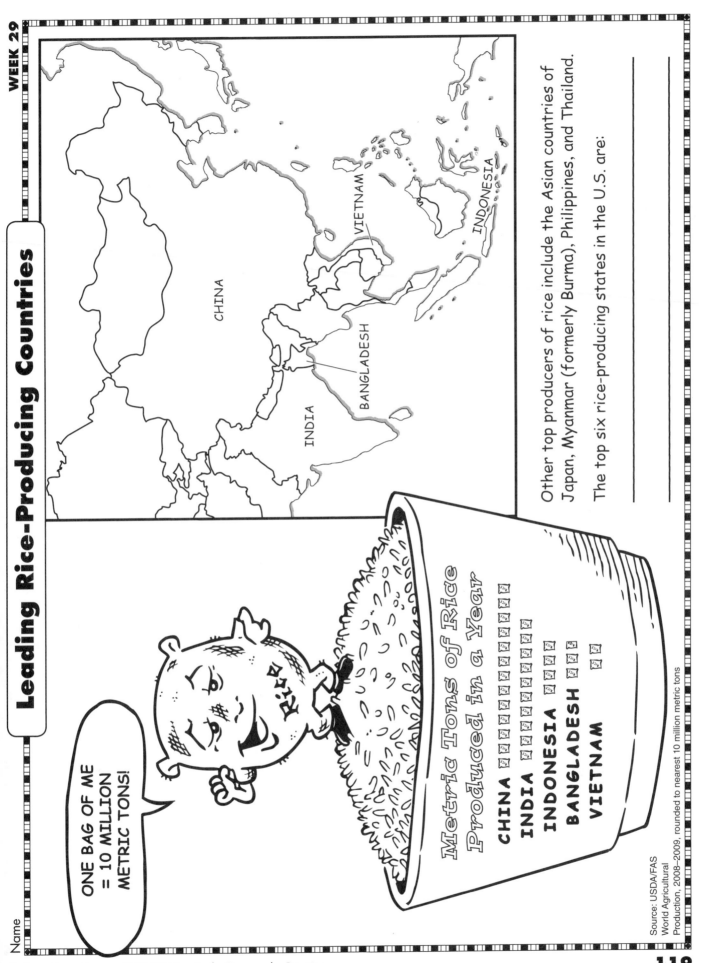

ONE BAG OF ME = 10 MILLION METRIC TONS!

Metric Tons of Rice Produced in a Year

CHINA 🌾🌾🌾🌾🌾🌾🌾🌾🌾🌾🌾🌾🌾🌾🌾🌾🌾🌾🌾
INDIA 🌾🌾🌾🌾🌾🌾🌾🌾🌾🌾
INDONESIA 🌾🌾🌾
BANGLADESH 🌾🌾
VIETNAM 🌾🌾

Other top producers of rice include the Asian countries of Japan, Myanmar (formerly Burma), Philippines, and Thailand.

The top six rice-producing states in the U.S. are:

_____

Source: USDA/FAS
World Agricultural
Production, 2008–2009, rounded to nearest 10 million metric tons

Leading Rice-Producing Countries

Monday

1. What information is given on the map and the chart?

    _____

    _____

2. Which parts of Asia are known for rice production?

    _____

Tuesday

1. Which country was and still is the top producer of rice? How much rice
    was produced in this country in 2008–2009?

    _____

2. Which two countries together produced 230 million metric tons of rice?

    _____

Wednesday

1. Which group of countries produced more rice—India, Indonesia, and
    Bangladesh, or China and Vietnam?

    _____

2. Name the other Asian countries, <u>not</u> included on the chart, that are top
    producers of rice.

    _____

    _____

Leading Rice-Producing Countries   WEEK 29

Thursday

1. Why are Central Asia and Southeast Asia ideal places for growing rice?

    _____

    _____

2. Do Asian farmers produce about 50 percent, 75 percent, or 90 percent of the world's rice?

    _____

Friday

1. In hilly areas, farmers in Asia cut terraces into the sides of mountains to plant rice. How do farmers plant rice in the lowland areas?

    _____

    _____

2. Rice is the staple food for over half the people in the world. What is meant by that statement?

    _____

    _____

Challenge

The United States often makes the list of the top ten rice-producing countries. Name the top six rice-producing states in the U.S. Search the Internet for your answers. Write your answers on the map as another caption.

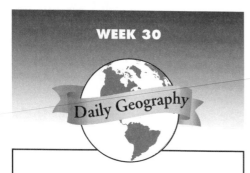

Boroughs of New York City

Introducing the Map

Share with students that New York City is the largest city in the United States. The 2010 census gave the population as 8,175,133. The people of New York City represent nearly all nationalities. Tell students the following background information about the peoples who settled the area:

The first people to settle in New York were several tribes from the Algonquian family of Native Americans. The first Europeans were the Dutch colonists who settled in the area in the 1600s. During the 1800s and early 1900s, millions of Europeans seeking a better life came to New York. During the mid-1900s, many black people from the southern states moved into the city. Also during this time, Spanish-speaking Americans from Puerto Rico came to New York. Since that time, immigrants from all over the world have poured into New York. Now it is one of the most culturally and ethnically diverse cities in the world. In fact, five ethnic groups—Black, Irish, Italian, Jewish, and Puerto Rican—make up 80 percent of the population.

Show students the map of New York City. Talk about how the city is divided into five areas called boroughs. Share the following information about each of these areas:

- Manhattan is the smallest in land area and the oldest borough. Manhattan has giant skyscrapers and is an important world center of commerce.

- The borough of Brooklyn has the largest population in New York City. It is an important port and industrial center. The Brooklyn, Manhattan, and Williamsburg bridges link the two boroughs.

- The Bronx is north of Manhattan and is chiefly a residential area.

- Queens is the largest borough in terms of area. It is linked to the other boroughs by busy expressways and subways.

- Staten Island has the smallest population. Staten Island ferries carry people to and from the mainland.

Introducing Vocabulary

borough any of the five political divisions of New York City

diverse varied

ethnic having to do with a group of people sharing the same national origins, language, or culture

port a harbor where ships can dock or anchor safely

ANSWER KEY

Monday
1. Brooklyn, Bronx, Manhattan, Queens, and Staten Island
2. 8,175,133; First in population, so it is the largest city in the U.S.

Tuesday
1. Bronx
2. Brooklyn; 2,504,700

Wednesday
1. Brooklyn
2. Queens

Thursday
1. Statue of Liberty
2. Ellis Island

Friday
1. Manhattan
2. Bronx

Challenge
Answers will vary, but students should draw the statue and write four facts. Examples of facts: The statue stands on Liberty Island. It is a huge copper statue of a woman wearing a crown. She is carrying a tablet and holding a torch. She is 151 feet (46 m) tall, situated on a five-star base.

Boroughs of New York City

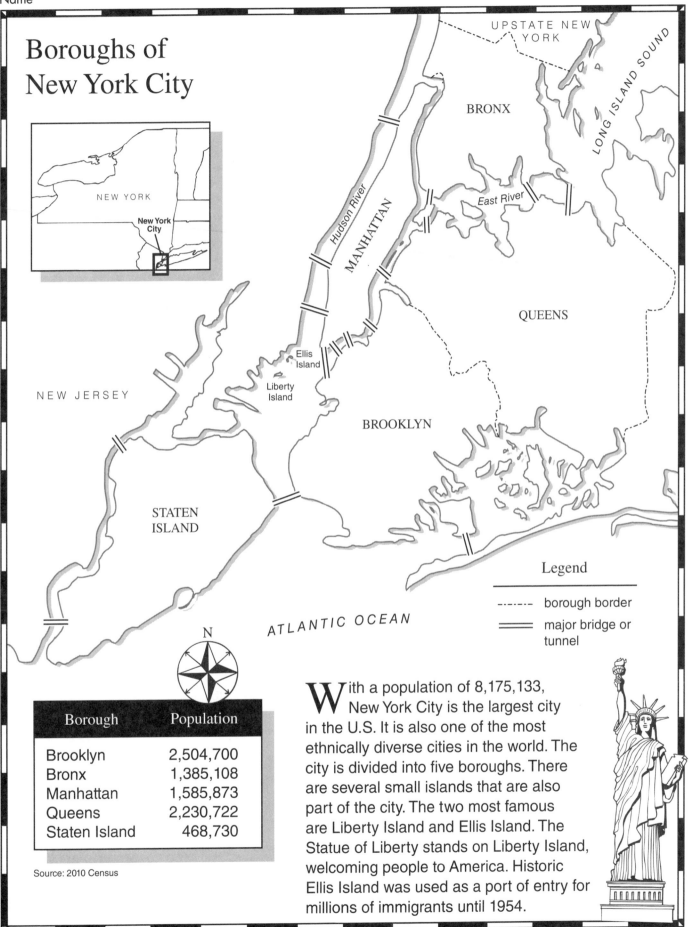

NEW YORK

New York City

UPSTATE NEW YORK

LONG ISLAND SOUND

BRONX

Hudson River

MANHATTAN

East River

QUEENS

Ellis Island

Liberty Island

NEW JERSEY

BROOKLYN

STATEN ISLAND

ATLANTIC OCEAN

N

Legend

- - - - - borough border

===== major bridge or tunnel

Borough	Population
Brooklyn	2,504,700
Bronx	1,385,108
Manhattan	1,585,873
Queens	2,230,722
Staten Island	468,730

Source: 2010 Census

With a population of 8,175,133, New York City is the largest city in the U.S. It is also one of the most ethnically diverse cities in the world. The city is divided into five boroughs. There are several small islands that are also part of the city. The two most famous are Liberty Island and Ellis Island. The Statue of Liberty stands on Liberty Island, welcoming people to America. Historic Ellis Island was used as a port of entry for millions of immigrants until 1954.

Boroughs of New York City

Monday

1. New York City is divided into five areas called boroughs. Name the five boroughs.

   _____

   _____

2. What is the population of New York City? What is its ranking among all cities in the United States?

   _____

Tuesday

1. Manhattan is famous for its giant skyscrapers. Which borough is northeast of Manhattan?

   _____

2. Which borough has the largest population? What is its population?

   _____

Wednesday

1. Staten Island is the only borough not directly connected to Manhattan. Staten Island is linked by bridge to which other borough?

   _____

2. Which borough is the largest in area and second-largest in population?

   _____

Boroughs of New York City

Thursday

1. Liberty Island is home to which famous landmark?

_____

2. Prior to 1954, where did immigrants have to go to enter New York City?

_____

Friday

1. Central Park, the Empire State Building, and the United Nations headquarters are all located in which borough of 1.6 million people?

_____

2. Which borough is the only one not separated from upstate New York by water?

_____

Challenge

The Statue of Liberty is located on an island in New York Harbor. She is a symbol of the United States that stands for freedom. Millions of immigrants have passed by the Statue of Liberty as they entered the United States.

On a piece of paper, draw a picture of the Statue of Liberty and write four facts to describe this famous landmark. Attach the paper to the map. Use an encyclopedia or other resource to help you.

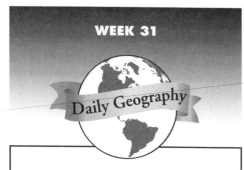

Time Zones of the United States

Introducing the Map

Ask students what it would be like if every community in the United States used a different time. The obvious answer is that people would be confused and many problems would be created. To avoid this confusion, a cooperative system was designed called standard time zones. Talk about the advantages of having regional time zones.

Explain the concept of time zones. A day is 24 hours long—the time it takes Earth to complete one rotation on its axis. Earth is divided into 24 time zones. The United States is divided into six of those 24 time zones.

Show students the "Time Zones of the United States." Tell students that each zone uses a time one hour different from its neighboring zones. The hours are earlier to the west of each zone and later to the east.

Go over all the names of the time zones and have students notice the one hour difference between each of them. Talk about how Alaska is so large that it is in two time zones. Explain that some of the Aleutian Islands of Alaska are so far west that scientists have grouped them with Hawaii, thus creating Hawaii-Aleutian Time.

Ask students in which time zone Chicago, Illinois, is. They will say Central Time. Then ask them: If it is 3:00 P.M. in Chicago, what time is it in Denver? The answer is 2:00 P.M. Ask students a couple more questions, each time changing the local times to help students understand the concept.

Extend the lesson to discuss daylight saving time. This is a plan in which clocks are set one hour ahead of standard time for a specified period of time. The plan provides for an additional hour of daylight. It begins on the second Sunday in March and ends on the first Sunday in November. Most states choose to go on daylight saving time, but several don't. Talk about how that complicates things.

Introducing Vocabulary

daylight saving time a plan in which clocks are set one hour ahead of standard time for a specific period of time

standard time zone a region in which the same time is used; Earth is divided into 24 time zones

ANSWER KEY

Monday
1. 6; Hawaii-Aleutian, Alaskan, Pacific, Mountain, Central, and Eastern
2. one hour

Tuesday
1. earlier
2. Eastern Time Zone

Wednesday
1. Hawaii-Aleutian Time Zone
2. 11:00 A.M.

Thursday
1. 10:00 P.M.
2. North Dakota, South Dakota, Nebraska, Kansas, and Texas

Friday
1. No, it's 2:00 A.M. and your grandfather is probably sleeping.
2. It is daylight saving time.

Challenge
Answers will vary, but students should make up two questions and provide answers to the questions.

Time Zones of the United States

Name

Daylight saving time begins on the second Sunday in March and ends on the first Sunday in November. Remember this trick to set your clocks one hour ahead in the spring and one hour back in the fall: spring ahead; fall back.

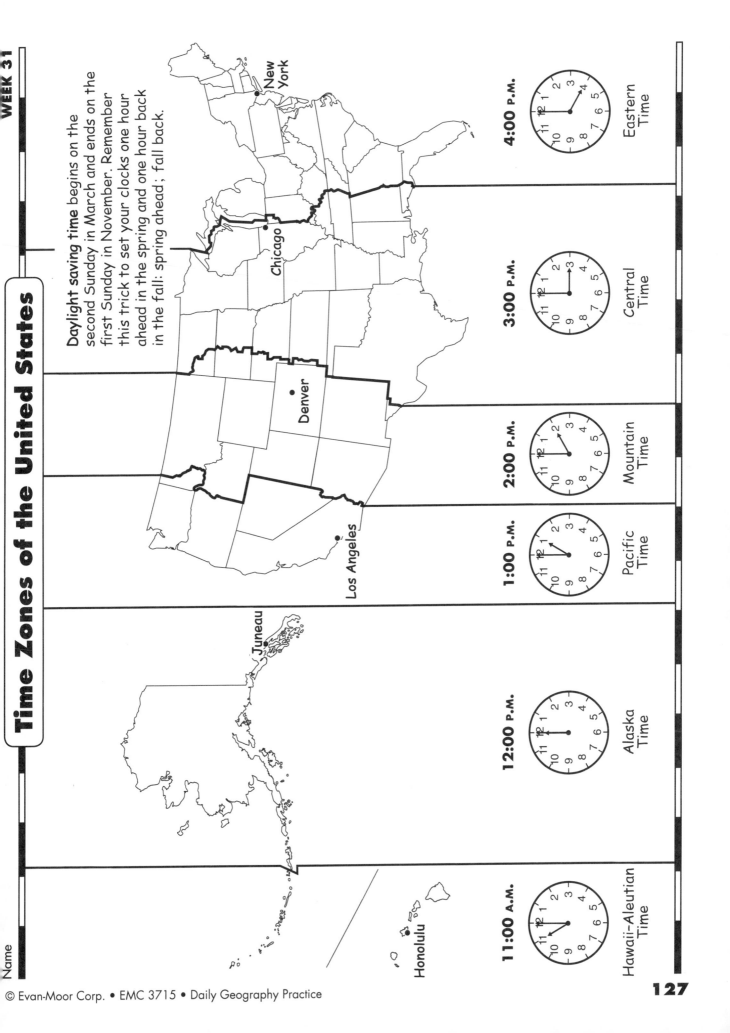

New York

Chicago

Denver

Los Angeles

Juneau

Honolulu

11:00 A.M.
Hawaii–Aleutian Time

12:00 P.M.
Alaska Time

1:00 P.M.
Pacific Time

2:00 P.M.
Mountain Time

3:00 P.M.
Central Time

4:00 P.M.
Eastern Time

Time Zones of the United States

Monday

1. The United States is divided into how many standard time zones? Name them from west to east.

   _____

   _____

2. What is the time difference between each time zone?

   _____

Tuesday

1. Are the hours earlier or later to the west of each time zone?

   _____

2. Cities in the Northeast region are part of which time zone?

   _____

Wednesday

1. Which time zone includes Hawaii and some of the western islands of Alaska?

   _____

2. If it is 1:00 P.M. in Chicago, what time is it in Los Angeles?

   _____

Time Zones of the United States

Thursday

1. If it is midnight in Chicago, what time is it in Seattle, Washington?

    _____

2. Which states have areas that are part of the Central and Mountain Time Zones?

    _____

    _____

Friday

1. If you live in Honolulu and it is 9:00 P.M., is it a good time to call your grandfather in New York? Why or why not?

    _____

2. It is the second Sunday in March and clocks have been set one hour ahead. Why?

    _____

Challenge

Make up two time zone questions. Write your questions on the back of the map page. Don't forget to include the answers. Pair up with a classmate and ask each other the time zone questions.

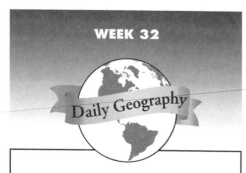

WEEK 32

Daily Geography

A Land Use Map: The North-Central Region

Introducing the Map

Define the term *land use* for students. Tell students that the North-Central region of the United States is used primarily for agricultural use. Show students the land use map for the North-Central region. Use the inset map to identify the location of this region in relation to the rest of the United States and Canada. Talk about the climate and types of landforms found in these states. As you define the terms in the legend, have students locate the areas of each type of land use on the map.

Students should notice that all of the states in the North-Central region have areas of cropland identified as "Cropland" or "Partly Cropland." Inform students that some of the major crops grown in these states are corn, soybeans, hay, wheat, dry beans, sugar beets, and potatoes. Iowa leads all the states in corn production, and Kansas leads the nation in wheat production.

Have students identify the states with forestland—Indiana, Michigan, Minnesota, Missouri, Ohio, South Dakota, and Wisconsin. Point out the small area of forestland in the western part of South Dakota. Forests cover only 4 percent of the land in South Dakota. Forests, however, cover more than half of Michigan. It is the second-largest grower of Christmas trees.

Next, locate the areas of grazing land in Kansas, Nebraska, North Dakota, and South Dakota. Talk about the livestock animals that are raised in these areas—beef and dairy cattle, hogs, lambs, turkeys, and sheep. Kansas is a leader in the production of beef cattle. In Wisconsin, dairy farming is the leading agricultural industry.

Explain that unproductive land is not suitable for cropland, forests, or grazing. Point out the small area of unproductive land in northern Minnesota. Discuss reasons why this area might be considered unproductive.

Introducing Vocabulary

cropland land used regularly for production of crops

grazing land a field covered with grass suitable for feeding livestock

land use the range of uses of Earth's surface made by humans; includes such uses as agricultural, industrial, open space, forestry, recreational, and residential

unproductive land land not usable for crops, grazing, or forests

---

ANSWER KEY

Monday
1. Land use in the North-Central region of the U.S.
2. 12; 12

Tuesday
1. 4; Kansas, Nebraska, North Dakota, and South Dakota
2. Indiana, Michigan, Minnesota, Missouri, Ohio, South Dakota, and Wisconsin; South Dakota

Wednesday
1. not suitable for cropland, forests, or for grazing; Minnesota
2. Illinois and Iowa

Thursday
1. Any two of the following: beef and dairy cattle, hogs, lambs, turkeys, or sheep
2. Any three of the following: corn, soybeans, hay, wheat, dry beans, sugar beets, and potatoes

Friday
1. agricultural
2. Minnesota, Michigan, and Wisconsin; cropland, partly cropland, and forests

Challenge
Students should add the following capitals to the map:
Springfield, IL; Indianapolis, IN; Des Moines, IA; Topeka, KS; Lansing, MI; St. Paul, MN; Jefferson City, MO; Lincoln, NE; Bismarck, ND; Columbus, OH; Pierre, SD; Madison, WI

A Land Use Map: The North-Central Region

Name

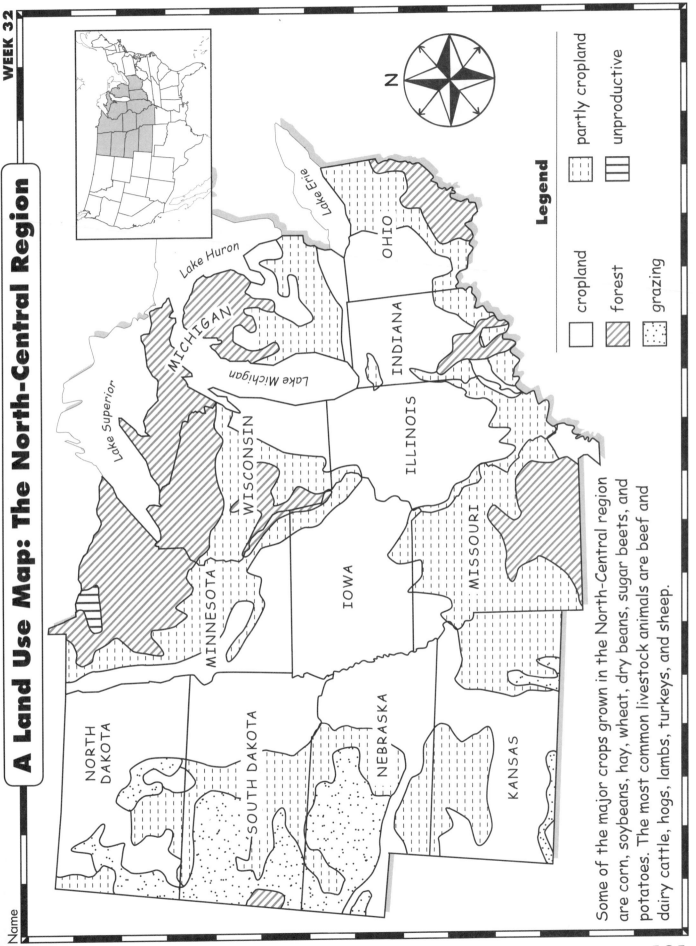

Some of the major crops grown in the North-Central region are corn, soybeans, hay, wheat, dry beans, sugar beets, and potatoes. The most common livestock animals are beef and dairy cattle, hogs, lambs, turkeys, and sheep.

Legend

☐	cropland	⬚	partly cropland
▨	forest	⬚	unproductive
⬚	grazing		

A Land Use Map:
The North-Central Region

Monday

1. What information is shown on the map?

   _____

2. How many states are shown on the map? How many of them have usable cropland?

   _____

Tuesday

1. How many states have good grazing lands for livestock? Name them.

   _____

   _____

2. Which states have forests? Of these, which state has the least amount of forestland?

   _____

   _____

Wednesday

1. What does the term *unproductive land* mean? Which state has a very small percentage of unproductive land?

   _____

2. Which states have only cropland for land use?

   _____

A Land Use Map: The North-Central Region

Thursday

1. Name two livestock animals found on large ranches and on grazing lands.

   _____

2. Name three major crops that are grown in the North-Central region.

   _____

   _____

Friday

1. Is land use in the North-Central region mostly agricultural, industrial, or open space?

   _____

2. Which states border Lake Superior? Which land use categories do they all have in common?

   _____

   _____

Challenge

Add the capitals of the states in the correct places on the map of the North-Central region. Use a reference political map to place the capitals in the correct positions.

WEEK 33

Daily Geography

A Tourist Map: Missouri

Introducing the Map

Review with students political and physical maps. Talk about a third kind of map called a geopolitical map. Tell students that people like to look at these kinds of maps when visiting places. Geopolitical maps can show where cities are located, natural features in the area, and human-made structures such as tourist attractions.

Ask students to name a state they would like to visit and why. An example might be the state of California. Students may point out cities they would like to visit such as Los Angeles or San Francisco. Natural features might include such places as beaches along the coast or Yosemite National Park. Human-made structures might include such things as the Golden Gate Bridge or Disneyland.

Explain to students that the physical features of a state help to determine what kinds of tourist attractions are possible. Show students the tourist map of Missouri. Students will notice that rivers dominate the state. Talk about the kinds of recreational opportunities rivers provide such as boating, fishing, and swimming. The Lake of the Ozarks is a popular resort and recreation center. There are more than 5,600 caves in Missouri. The Meramec Caverns is a series of huge caves that many people visit.

Ask students which tourist attractions are human-made structures. They should point out such things as the Gateway Arch, Harry S. Truman Library, George Washington Carver's monument, and Mark Twain's home. These structures have historical significance. St. Louis is especially significant because it served as a gateway to the West and as a main port for the Mississippi River steamboats. Lewis and Clark started their journey to the Pacific Northwest at St. Louis, as did pioneers heading west. Be sure to read the "fun facts" with students.

Tell students that each state has a Division of Tourism. This agency is responsible for the business of tourism. In Missouri, tourism is the state's second-largest industry. Remind students that only a sampling of tourist attractions have been included on this map. You may wish to extend this lesson to have students research the labeled tourist attractions or add others to the map.

Introducing Vocabulary

geopolitical map shows political and physical features on one map

tourism tourist travel, especially when regarded as a source of income for a state or country

ANSWER KEY

Monday
1. rivers such as the Missouri and Mississippi, caves such as Meramec Caverns, Lake of the Ozarks, and a national forest
2. Harry S. Truman, Mark Twain, and George Washington Carver

Tuesday
1. It has five levels, and one of the caves is large enough to hold 300 cars. It was a hideout for the outlaw Jesse James.
2. St. Joseph, MO, and Sacramento, CA

Wednesday
1. Branson; southwestern Missouri
2. Harry S. Truman Library; It is President Truman's library, which houses over three million historic documents.

Thursday
1. Mark Twain was a famous writer who wrote *Tom Sawyer* and *Huckleberry Finn*. He was born and raised in Missouri.
2. St. Louis; The Gateway Arch commemorates St. Louis's role in the settlement of the West. Lewis and Clark started their journey in St. Louis, as did many pioneers.

Friday
1. There are 5,600 recorded caves featuring stalactites, stalagmites, cave life, and fossil remains.
2. shows both political and physical features on the same map

Challenge
Answers will vary.

A Tourist Map: Missouri

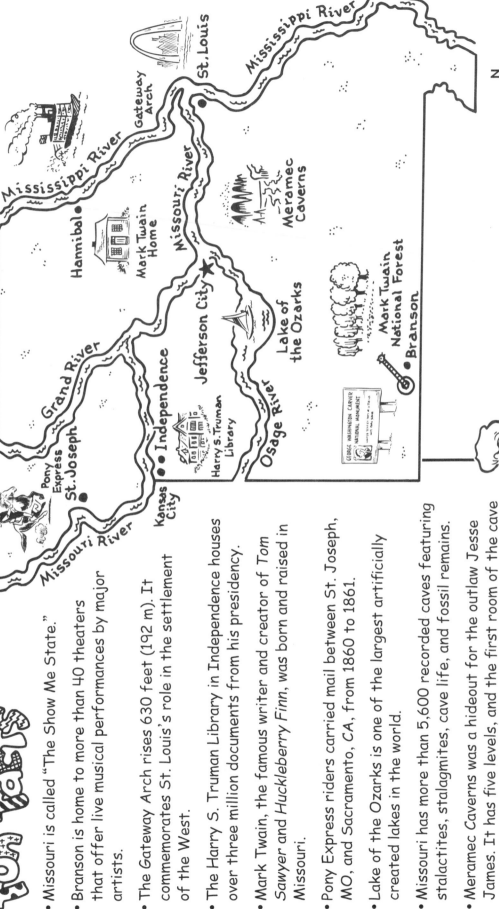

Fun Facts

- Missouri is called "The Show Me State."

- Branson is home to more than 40 theaters that offer live musical performances by major artists.

- The Gateway Arch rises 630 feet (192 m). It commemorates St. Louis's role in the settlement of the West.

- The Harry S. Truman Library in Independence houses over three million documents from his presidency.

- Mark Twain, the famous writer and creator of *Tom Sawyer* and *Huckleberry Finn*, was born and raised in Missouri.

- Pony Express riders carried mail between St. Joseph, MO, and Sacramento, CA, from 1860 to 1861.

- Lake of the Ozarks is one of the largest artificially created lakes in the world.

- Missouri has more than 5,600 recorded caves featuring stalactites, stalagmites, cave life, and fossil remains.

- Meramec Caverns was a hideout for the outlaw Jesse James. It has five levels, and the first room of the cave is large enough to hold 300 cars.

- George Washington Carver, a famous scientist who made more than 300 products from peanuts, was born a slave on a farm in Missouri.

A Tourist Map: Missouri

Monday

1. Name three physical features that help make Missouri a major tourist state.

   _____

   _____

2. Name three famous Americans who have historic buildings or monuments named after them in Missouri.

   _____

Tuesday

1. Why do people visit the Meramec Caverns?

   _____

2. Pony Express riders could make the 1,966-mile (3,164-km) journey in 10 days or less. Which cities did they travel to and from?

   _____

Wednesday

1. Which city is noted for its musical entertainment value? In which part of the state is the city located?

   _____

2. Which historic site is located in Independence, MO? Write a fact about this site.

   _____

   _____

Name _____

Daily Geography

A Tourist Map: Missouri

Thursday

1. Mark Twain has a cave and a national forest named after him. Why?

   _____

   _____

2. The Gateway Arch is considered a historic site. Where is it located, and why is the monument historically significant?

   _____

   _____

Friday

1. Why is Missouri called a "spelunker's paradise"?

   _____

   _____

2. The tourist map of Missouri is also called a geopolitical map. What is a geopolitical map?

   _____

   _____

Challenge

Missouri has several nicknames—Cave State, Mother of the West, Ozark State, and the Show Me State.

You have been assigned to promote tourism in Missouri. Decide which nickname is the best and design a logo for it. Draw your logo on the map page.

WEEK 34

Daily Geography

A Resource Map: Mexico's Minerals

Introducing the Map

Ask students to name a natural resource. Students may say resources such as air, water, and land. Tell students that natural resources include those things, but that there are also mineral natural resources on Earth. Mineral resources include such things as coal, oil, stone, and sand. Mineral resources also include precious metals such as gold and silver. Mineral fuels—coal, oil, and natural gas—provide heat, light, and power to many people. Explain that mineral fuels are also called fossil fuels.

Tell students that Mexico has a wide variety of valuable minerals. Show students the map of Mexico as you share the following information with them. Also, be sure to read the facts that are given on the map page as well.

> Mexico ranks first in the world for the production of silver. An estimated one-fifth to one-third of all silver that has been recovered from the Earth has come from Mexico. Mexico now mines about a sixth of the world's annual production of silver. Most of the silver mines are found in the central regions of Mexico.
>
> The country also has large deposits of copper, gold, lead, iron ore, and zinc. Large iron ore deposits help Mexico's growing steel industry.
>
> Mexico produces the mineral fossil fuels of coal, natural gas, and oil. Mexico's economy depends mostly on oil. Mexico is a major exporter of petroleum products. Petroleum and petroleum products make up more than a third of Mexico's earnings from foreign trade.
>
> Mexico also mines large quantities of salt and sulfur and other valuable minerals such as fluorite, manganese, and mercury. However, these minerals are not shown on the map.

Introducing Vocabulary

crude oil yellow-to-black oil as it occurs naturally in a reservoir

economy the way a state or country develops, distributes, and uses its money, goods, and services

export to send products to another country to be sold there

fossil fuels mineral fuels of coal, oil, and natural gas

mineral a natural substance such as copper, gold, and salt

natural resources materials supplied by nature that are useful or necessary for life

petroleum another name for oil

ANSWER KEY

Monday
1. silver; 7
2. lead–6 and zinc–6; inland

Tuesday
1. 4; 1 on the Peninsula of Lower California, 2 in northwestern Mexico, and 1 in central Mexico
2. 2; north-central and central Mexico

Wednesday
1. coal, oil, and natural gas
2. along the Gulf of Mexico coastline; Mexico and the U.S.

Thursday
1. Coal is produced in southwest Mexico on the coastline of the Pacific Ocean, and natural gas is found on the coast of the Bay of Campeche and northeast Mexico along the border of the Gulf of Mexico.
2. oil, or petroleum; Mexico pumps more than 1 billion barrels of petroleum each year.

Friday
1. iron ore; along the central coast of the Pacific Ocean
2. *Export* is to send products to another country to be sold there; profits and the jobs created from the sale of exports help Mexico's economy.

Challenge
Students should write the paragraph about exports and include the United States as Mexico's number one trade partner.

Name

A Resource Map: Mexico's Minerals

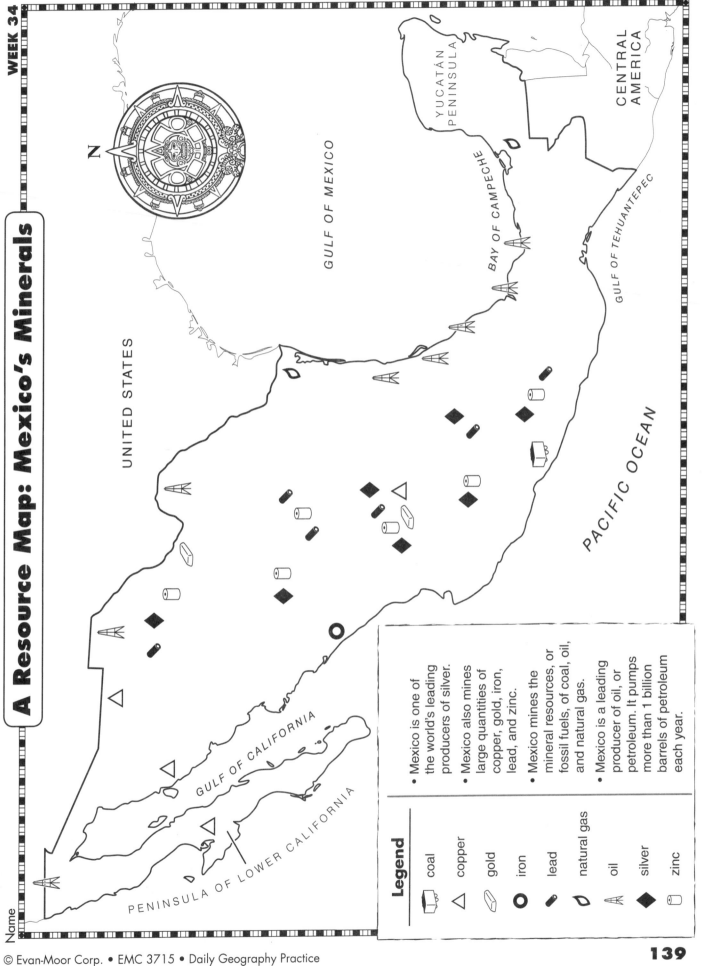

UNITED STATES

GULF OF MEXICO

YUCATÁN PENINSULA

BAY OF CAMPECHE

GULF OF TEHUANTEPEC

CENTRAL AMERICA

PACIFIC OCEAN

GULF OF CALIFORNIA

PENINSULA OF LOWER CALIFORNIA

N

- Mexico is one of the world's leading producers of silver.
- Mexico also mines large quantities of copper, gold, iron, lead, and zinc.
- Mexico mines the mineral resources, or fossil fuels, of coal, oil, and natural gas.
- Mexico is a leading producer of oil, or petroleum. It pumps more than 1 billion barrels of petroleum each year.

Legend

coal	
copper	
gold	
iron	
lead	
natural gas	
oil	
silver	
zinc	

A Resource Map: Mexico's Minerals

Monday

1. Mexico is the world's leading producer of which mineral? How many areas of Mexico produce this mineral?

   _____

2. How many areas produce the minerals lead and zinc? Are the deposits of these two minerals located mostly along the coast or inland?

   _____

Tuesday

1. How many areas produce copper? In which areas of Mexico is copper mined?

   _____

2. How many areas in Mexico produce gold? In which locations are these deposits of gold?

   _____

Wednesday

1. Which of the minerals shown on the map are called mineral fuels, or fossil fuels?

   _____

2. Where are most of the oil wells found in Mexico? Three oil well symbols can be found on the border of which two countries?

   _____

A Resource Map: Mexico's Minerals

Thursday

1. Oil is produced along the northern border and the Gulf of Mexico border. Where are the other two fossil fuels found in Mexico?

_____

_____

2. The economy of Mexico depends greatly on one of the fossil fuels. Which fossil fuel is it? Give a statistic about this fossil fuel.

_____

Friday

1. Which mineral helps to support Mexico's growing steel industry? Where is this mineral located in Mexico?

_____

2. Mexico's leading exports include petroleum, copper, salt, sulfur, silver, and zinc. What does *export* mean, and how do exports help Mexico?

_____

_____

Challenge

In 2009, Mexico's mineral exports, excluding petroleum and natural gas, were about $5 billion.

Research to find out which country is Mexico's most valued trade partner for these minerals. Write the above facts and the new information on the back of the map.

A History Map: Ancient Greece

Introducing the Map

Share with students that historical maps are specialized maps that give information about an earlier time in history. People have been making maps for thousands of years. Ancient mapmakers were able to make fairly accurate maps of the areas they knew well. Information from explorers and traders helped early cartographers to improve their maps. Navigational tools such as the compass and the astrolabe helped ancient sailors to determine location and distance.

From those ancient maps and historical records, modern cartographers are able to show ancient civilizations on maps. Show students the map of ancient Greece. Share with students that ancient Greece consisted chiefly of a mountainous peninsula that reached into the Mediterranean Sea, nearby islands, and the west coast of Asia Minor, which is now part of Turkey. The peninsula made up mainland Greece. The mainland separated two arms of the Mediterranean, which are called the Aegean and Ionian Seas. A narrow strip of land called Peloponnesus linked the southern part of the mainland to the northern part.

Tell students that some of the major regions of ancient Greece are shown in capital letters, and the city-states are designated with dots. Share with students that city-states consisted of a city or town and the surrounding villages and farmland. The Greek city-states were fiercely independent and often fought among themselves. The best known city-states were Athens and Sparta. The city-states never became united as one nation. They did, however, share a common language, religion, and culture.

Also, share with students that throughout ancient Greece's history—from about 3,000 B.C. to 146 B.C.— the civilization gained and lost territories. The Romans conquered Greece in 146 B.C., and Greece did not become an independent nation again until the early 1800s.

Introducing Vocabulary

ancient civilization a very old, complex society with a stable food supply, specialization of labor, a government, and a highly developed culture

cartographer mapmaker

city-state a self-governing unit made up of a city and its surrounding villages and farmland

history map a map that shows places or events from the past

ANSWER KEY

Monday
1. Aegean, Ionian, and the Mediterranean Seas
2. Any five of the following: Athens, Delphi, Marathon, Olympia, Mycenae, Piraeus, Sparta, Thebes, and Thermopylae

Tuesday
1. Peloponnesus
2. Crete

Wednesday
1. Athens
2. Mount Olympus

Thursday
1. Olympia
2. Marathon

Friday
1. a city and the surrounding villages and farmland
2. Salamis

Challenge
Students should add a caption to the map page. Some examples: Ancient Greece consisted chiefly of a mountainous peninsula that reached into the Mediterranean Sea, nearby islands, and the west coast of Asia Minor, which is now part of Turkey. The peninsula made up mainland Greece. The mainland separated two arms of the Mediterranean, which are called the Aegean and Ionian Seas. A narrow strip of land called Peloponnesus linked the southern part of the mainland to the northern part.

A History Map:
Ancient Greece

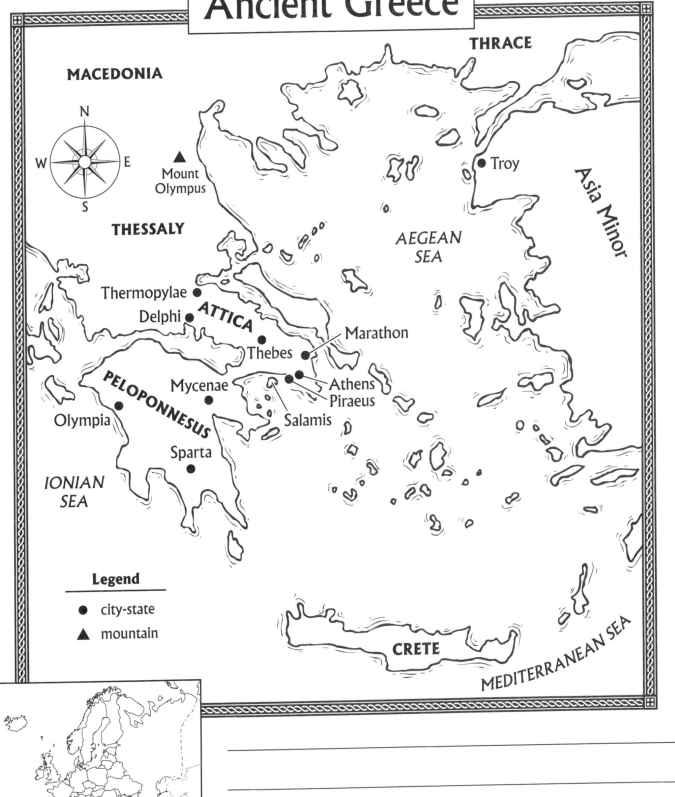

MACEDONIA

THRACE

N
W   E
S

Mount
Olympus

THESSALY

Troy

Asia Minor

AEGEAN
SEA

Thermopylae
Delphi   **ATTICA**
Thebes   Marathon

Athens
Piraeus
Salamis

PELOPONNESUS

Mycenae

Olympia

Sparta

IONIAN
SEA

Legend
● city-state
▲ mountain

CRETE

MEDITERRANEAN SEA

A History Map: Ancient Greece

Monday

1. Which seas surrounded ancient Greece?

   _____

2. The mainland of Greece was a peninsula. Name at least five city-states located on the mainland.

   _____

   _____

Tuesday

1. The city-states of Olympia and Sparta were part of which region?

   _____

2. The beginnings of the Greek civilization can be traced to the largest island in ancient Greece. Name the island.

   _____

Wednesday

1. Which city-state was named after the goddess Athena?

   _____

2. The ancient Greeks believed in gods and goddesses who made their home on a mountain. Name the Greek mountain.

   _____

Daily Geography

A History Map: Ancient Greece

Thursday

1. The first recorded ancient Olympic Games took place in which city-state in 776 B.C.?

   _____

2. A modern-day long-distance race is named after which city-state?

   _____

Friday

1. What three areas made up a city-state?

   _____

   _____

2. During a major battle, the Greeks sank half the Persian fleet off the coast of this island. Name this small island.

   _____

Challenge

Add a caption to the map describing the location of ancient Greece.

WEEK 36

Daily Geography

A City Plan

Introducing the Map

Ask students to name places in their town or city. They might name such places as a park, school, video store, or hospital. Discuss how hard and complicated it would be to plan a city. Where would the residential areas be? Would they build new neighborhood homes near parks or busy commercial areas? City leaders and planners have a lot to think about.

Remind students that cities grew from villages, to small towns, to larger cities over time. As a city grows, people have to think about the additional needs of the community. City planning involves the work of many people such as local government officials and citizen volunteers. City planners are hired to help. City planners are people who advise local governments on ways to improve the community.

City planners deal mostly with the physical layout of the community. They make proposals on ways to improve the city. Their proposals may include projects to build or replace run-down commercial or housing developments. They may include plans for new recreation areas, shopping centers, or ways to improve transportation routes.

The city planners come up with a master plan. The master plan shows how land should be used. It shows how public facilities and services such as schools and transportation systems should be improved or expanded.

Show students the map of a fictitious city. Talk about the different parts of the city. Read the index to see the different areas. Students should notice the undeveloped land area. Tell them the city planners have proposed to the city planning commission and city council that the land should be used as a landfill site. Talk about the pros and cons of such a proposal. Students will decide how to use the land on the challenge question.

Introducing Vocabulary

city planner a person who advises local governments on ways to improve the community

commercial area an area where businesses and stores are located

community services public places that provide for the needs of a community such as schools, hospitals, police stations, and parks

industrial area an area where factories or large industries are located

master plan a comprehensive plan that shows how land use of an area may be developed or improved

residential area an area where people's homes are located

Section	Area
1	Industrial area
2	Airport
3	Undeveloped land
4	Older residential area
5	New residential area
6	Bus station
7	City library
8	City park
9	Offices and apartments
10	Hospital
11	High school
12	Police station
13	Fire station
14	Elementary school
15	Gas station
16	Commercial area

A City Plan

Name

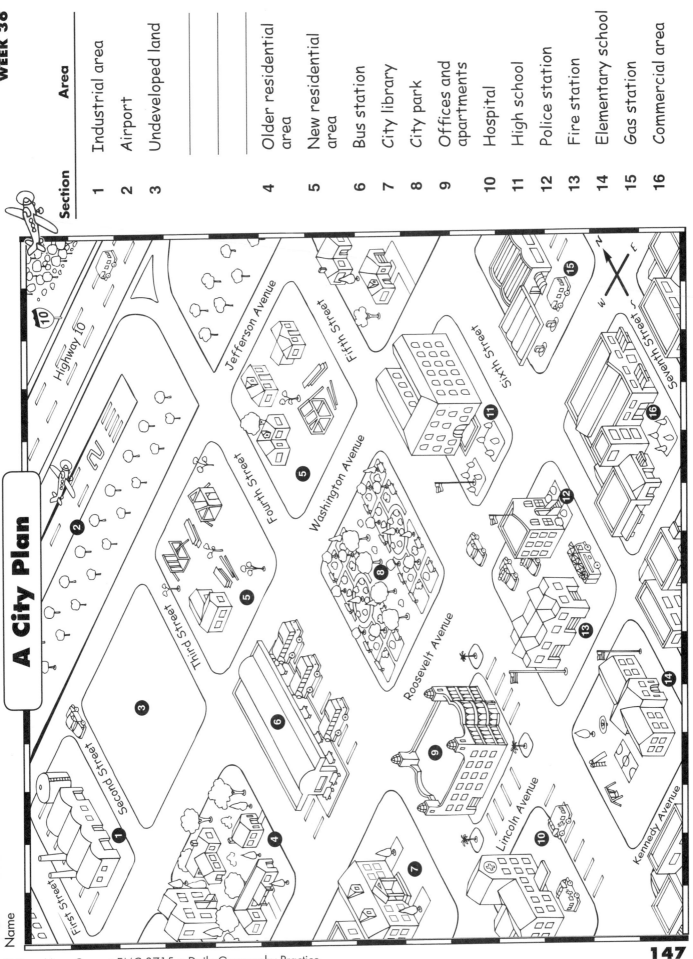

A City Plan

Monday

1. How many labeled areas provide housing? Which section has the newest houses?

   _____

2. Name the transportation systems shown on the map. Name another transportation system that may be in a city.

   _____

   _____

Tuesday

1. A large factory is in which section and area?

   _____

2. The city officials wanted the high school to be near a residential area. Was the plan followed? Why or why not?

   _____

   _____

Wednesday

1. Name at least five community service places that are shown on the map.

   _____

   _____

2. What kinds of buildings would be in a commercial area?

   _____

A City Plan

Thursday

1. What are the advantages and disadvantages about the location of the airport?

   _____

2. The city planner proposed that the city park be in the center of the city. Was that plan approved? How do you know?

   _____

Friday

1. How does the location of Highway 10 affect the housing development in a positive way and in a negative way?

   _____

   _____

2. Is the elementary school in a convenient location to most people's homes? Why or why not?

   _____

   _____

Challenge

Pretend you are a city official and you have just received a proposal from the city planner. She has recommended that the undeveloped land in the city be used for a new landfill site. Look at the city map and decide if this is a good site for a new landfill area.

1. Write your opinion on the back of the map page. Be sure to include the pros and cons of the proposal, and then make a decision one way or another.

2. Draw what you have planned for section 3 on the map.

3. Name the area in the space provided.

Geography
Glossary

belongs to:

_____

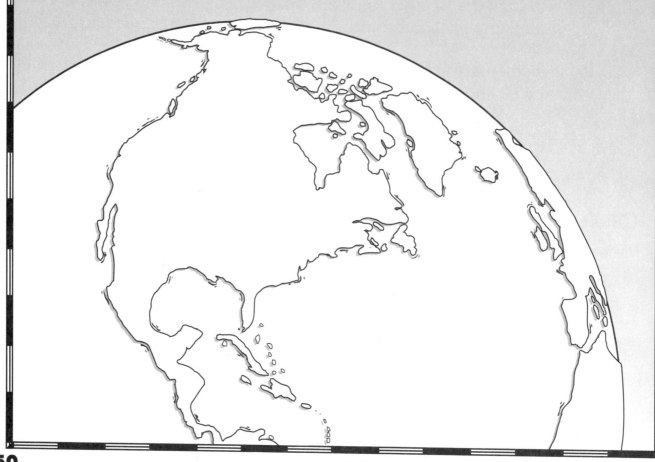

absolute location description of a place using grid coordinates (latitude and longitude)

agriculture the business of farming

air carrier airport airport that serves planes of commercial airlines

ancient civilization a very old complex society with a stable food supply, specialization of labor, a government, and a highly developed culture

archipelago a group of islands

Arctic Circle a line of latitude that runs through northern North America, northern Asia, and northern Europe (66.5°N latitude)

arctic climate a climate of extreme cold.

Arctic region region of continuous cold around the North Pole; includes Arctic Ocean, thousands of islands, and the northern parts of Asia, Europe, and North America

artesian basin land formed by underground water

bar scale a graphic that compares the distance on a map to the actual distance it represents, as in *one inch represents 100 miles*

basin land drained by a river

bight a bay formed by the curve of a coastline

biome a large area or environment that shares the same general climate of temperature and rainfall; different biomes support different types of plants and animals

borough any of the five political divisions of New York City

butte a flat-topped hill with steep sides; a column of rock

Canadian Shield a U-shaped region of ancient rock that curves around the Hudson Bay; southern part of shield is thick with forests and northern part is tundra

cape a point of land that extends into a sea or an ocean

capital a city in a country or state where the government is based

Capitol the building in Washington, D.C., occupied by the Congress of the U.S.

Capitol Hill the hill in Washington, D.C., on which stands the Capitol building

cardinal directions directions of north (N), south (S), east (E), and west (W)

cargo all freight, except baggage, carried by an airplane

cartographer mapmaker

census an official count of all the people living in a country or district

Central America a region of seven countries between Mexico and South America including Belize, Costa Rica, El Salvador, Guatemala, Honduras, Nicaragua, and Panama

city planner a person who advises local governments on ways to improve the community

city-state a self-governing unit made up of a city and its surrounding villages and farmland

climate usual weather in a particular place over a period of time

climate zone a region in which usual weather patterns occur over time

commercial area an area where businesses and stores are located

community services public places that provide for the needs of a community such as schools, hospitals, police stations, and parks

compass rose a directional arrow that shows cardinal and sometimes intermediate directions on a map

concourse a large open space for passage of crowds

contiguous sharing an edge or boundary; touching

control tower a glass-enclosed booth equipped with radar, radio, signal lights, and other equipment for directing air traffic

coordinates the latitude and longitude address of a place on a map

coral a substance made up of skeletons of tiny sea creatures

coral reef a ridge made of coral and other materials that have solidified into rock

cropland land used regularly for production of crops

crude oil yellow-to-black oil as it occurs naturally in a reservoir

cultural landmark a place selected and pointed out as important to a group of people

cultural map a map that shows patterns of ethnic groups, religious practices, languages spoken, educational levels, and recreational choices

culture language, beliefs, traditions, arts and crafts, political systems, and technologies of a group of people

daylight saving time a plan in which clocks are set one hour ahead of standard time for a specific period

degrees units of latitude or longitude (° is the symbol for degrees)

dependency land and waters controlled by a state, nation, or government

desert a dry region with little or no rainfall

District of Columbia (D.C.) an area of land controlled by the federal government

diverse varied

dune a mound or ridge of windblown sand

economy the way a state or country develops, distributes, and uses its money, goods, and services

ecosystem a community of animals and plants interacting with their environment

elevation height of the land above sea level

Ellipse an oval-shaped, park-like area in Washington, D.C.

equator an imaginary line that runs around the center of Earth, halfway between the North and South Poles at 0° latitude

equidistant projection projection that shows land and water in relation to a central point

erg a vast sea of sand

ethnic having to do with a group of people sharing the same national origins, language, or culture

Eurasia a landmass made up of the continents of Asia and Europe

export to send products to another country to be sold there

fossil fuels mineral fuels of coal, oil, and natural gas

gate an airport terminal entryway used for boarding or leaving an airplane

geographic grid the intersecting pattern formed by the lines of latitude and longitude

geopolitical map shows political and physical features on one map

grazing land a field covered with grass suitable for feeding livestock

Greater Antilles an island group of the West Indies including Cuba, Jamaica, Hispaniola (Dominican Republic and Haiti), and Puerto Rico (U.S.)

grid a pattern of lines that form squares

gulf a large area of ocean that is partly surrounded by land

hemisphere half of the Earth

highway interchange a place where major roads meet or join

history map a map that shows places or events from the past

index an alphabetical listing of place names on a map and the grid squares in which they are found

industrial area an area where factories or large industries are located

inset map a small map set within the border of a larger one

intermediate directions directions of northeast (NE), northwest (NW), southeast (SE), and southwest (SW)

international border a border between countries

interstate highway a major public road that is part of a nationwide highway system; the interstate highway system was created after the U.S. highway system

isthmus a narrow strip of land having water on each side and connecting two larger bodies of land

land use the range of uses of Earth's surface made by humans; includes such uses as agricultural, industrial, open space, forestry, recreational, and residential

legend (key) a list that explains the symbols on a map

Lesser Antilles an island group of the West Indies including eight countries and eight dependencies

lines of latitude (parallels) imaginary lines on Earth that run parallel to the equator

lines of longitude (meridians) imaginary lines on Earth that run between the North and South Poles

map sketch a rough drawing of a mental map

master plan a comprehensive plan that shows how land use of an area may be developed or improved

memorial something built to honor a person or an event, such as a monument or a statue

mental map a map that a person pictures in his or her mind

meridians (lines of longitude) imaginary lines on Earth that run between the North and South Poles

mesa a flat-topped hill with steep sides; larger than a butte

Middle East a large region that covers parts of northern Africa, southwestern Asia, and southeastern Europe

mileage total number of miles traveled

mineral a natural substance such as copper, gold, and salt

mountain any point of land that rises quickly to at least 1,000 feet above its surroundings

mountain peak the summit, or highest point, of a mountain

mountain range a group or chain of mountains

mountain system a group of mountain ranges

mouth the part of a river where it empties into another body of water

National Mall a public walkway in Washington, D.C.

national park an area set aside by a nation's government to protect natural beauty, wildlife, or other remarkable features

natural resources materials supplied by nature that are useful or necessary for life

nomad a person who moves from place to place looking for food, water, and grazing land for his livestock

North Pole the point on Earth located at 90 degrees (90°) north latitude, where the lines of longitude meet

oasis a place in the desert where there is a source of water and where plants grow

parallels (lines of latitude) imaginary lines on Earth that run parallel to the equator

passage another name for a channel; a body of water joining two larger bodies of water

petroleum another name for oil

physical map a map that shows natural landforms and waterways on Earth's surface

plains a large flat area of land

plateau a flat-topped hill with steep sides; larger than a mesa

polar projection a kind of equidistant projection that includes one of the poles as its center

political map a map that shows human-made features and boundaries such as cities, highways, and countries

population (populous) total number of people who live in a place

port a harbor where ships can dock or anchor safely

precipitation rain, snow, sleet, hail, or drizzle

prime meridian an imaginary line that runs from the North Pole to the South Pole of Earth at 0° longitude

product something that is made by a natural process

projection a system for mapping the round Earth on a flat surface

region an area of land or water with certain characteristics that make it different from other areas

relative location description of a place using the relation of one place to another

residential area an area where people's homes are located

rice paddy a rice field

river system a river and the smaller streams that supply water to the river

road map a map for motorists that shows the highways of an area

sand sea a vast region covered by sand and dunes

sea a body of salt water that is part of an ocean, yet is partially enclosed by land

source the place where a river begins

South Pole the point on Earth located at 90 degrees (90°) south latitude where the lines of longitude meet

standard time zone a region in which the same time is used; Earth is divided into 24 time zones

staple a basic food that is always produced and sold

statistic a fact or piece of information expressed as a number or percentage

strait a narrow channel connecting two bodies of water

tableland a high, broad, level plateau

temperate climate a climate without extremes of either cold or heat

terminal a main airport building for passenger services

tourism tourist travel, especially when regarded as a source of income for a state or country

traffic pattern a pattern of flight around an airport for arriving and departing aircraft

tributary a small stream or river that flows into a larger one

tropical climate a climate of heat and rain

unproductive land land not usable for crops, grazing, or forests

U.S. highway a major public road that is part of a nationwide highway system; the U.S. highway system was created before the interstate highway system

weather conditions in the Earth's atmosphere at a certain place and time

West Indies an island chain that divides the Caribbean Sea from the rest of the Atlantic Ocean

My Glossary Words

As you work through the weekly maps, you may find other words that are new to you. Write the definitions of those words on this page.

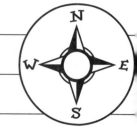